How to Feel Like A Somebody Again

Dale Galloway

HARVEST HOUSE PUBLISHERS
Irvine, California 92714

Verses marked TLB are from THE LIVING BIBLE, copyright 1971, Tyndale House Publishers, Wheaton, Illinois. Used by permission.

Verses marked NASB are from the NEW AMERICAN STANDARD BIBLE, copyright The Lockman Foundation 1960, 1962, 1963, 1968, 1971, 1972, 1973, 1975 and are used by permission.

HOW TO FEEL LIKE A SOMEBODY AGAIN

Copyright © 1978 Harvest House Publishers
Irvine, California 92714
Library of Congress Catalog Card Number 78-55587
ISBN #0-89081-130-X

Printed in the United States of America.

DEDICATION

I dedicate this book to a very special person:
   my mother, Clara Belle Sherman Galloway
Who has never stopped believing in me as a person.
Who, at the age of seventy—when left alone—
   dared to begin to live again by founding a
   new ministry for senior citizens in her town.
   Interestingly, it is called the J-O-Y Club,
   which she tells me means "Just Old Youth."

ADDITIONAL BOOKS
by the author

Dream a New Dream, Tyndale House Publishers
You Can Win with Love, Harvest House Publishers
We're Making Our Home a Happy Place, Tyndale House
   Publishers
There Is a Solution to Your Money Problems, Regal Books

CONTENTS

Introduction

It shocked me when the lady told me that what I had said made her cry all day and most of an agonizing night. While working at trying to keep my outward composure, on the inside I was asking, "Dear God—what on earth did I say? Here all these years I have taken pride in putting new wings of hope on sagging, weary spirits, and now I have deeply wounded this dear woman."

Further questioning revealed that the hurting lady had not even heard my well-prepared and polished speech. She confided that all she heard were the first words and, at that point, she had been overcome by an uncontrollable flood of tears.

Throughout the remainder of the counseling session my curiosity was aroused as to what I had said in the opening words of the speech. The instant she left my office I jumped up to my file cabinet, yanked out the drawer and grabbed the notes from my talk. Here are the opening words that had hit her like a ton of bricks: "Do You Ever Feel Worthless?"

At one time or another, I guess everyone of us has experienced the devastating, defeating feelings of worthlessness. It is also true that an overwhelming majority of people alive today feel like they are "a nobody."

Unfortunately there are many things which can make a good person feel like a nobody. Things like: the cold, competitive impersonal society that we all live in; a childhood marred by negative remarks and lacking in love; a guilt-ridden conscience locked into self-condemnation; deep inner hurts that have gone unhealed; faulty and negative thinking; past failures; and a lack of purpose and goals. Whatever the cause or causes, a poor self-image is the most difficult kind of bondage to live under. It is the heaviest of burdens to carry. No greater load!

. Wherever a person goes, how he thinks and feels about himself goes along. From one's own self-image there is no escape. But because Jesus lives, there is hope, and inner healing for everyone. Believe it, a new you is just waiting to be reborn, and to bloom into full beauty.

Believe it—

A rebirth of self-worth awaits you,

A fresh new start is knocking at your door,

An opportunity to discover your better self is here,

A healing for your yet unhealed hurts is about to happen,

A release to experience love is on the way,

A turning of your past failures into future blessings is now ready to begin.

And now for all of you who long to feel once again like a somebody, I share with you—HOW TO.

1

✦⊱❀⊰✦

What Do You Do When You Feel Like A Nobody?

1

❧◈❧

Courageously Jim and Kathy had sacrificed to put him through law school. Together they had struggled through the lean years while Jim was beginning his law practice. Now fifteen years into the marriage, four children later—just when Jim has become one of the foremost attorneys in the city, and for the first time they are enjoying financial freedom—suddenly Kathy is suffering an identity crisis. It seemed that the more successful Jim becomes, the more she feels like a nobody. She wants to know, "What do you do when you feel like a nobody?"

Roland is a 32-year-old swinging single. You name the place and he has been there. You name it and he's done it. Recently he has been suffering from long periods of depression. Last night after picking up a strange woman at a bar and having physical relations with her, he felt so crummy about himself as a person that he came ever so close to committing suicide. Fed up with shallow physical relationships that leave him feeling alone and like a nobody, he wants to know, "What can I do to get my life straightened out and to feel like a somebody again?"

At age 31 I was fulfilling my boyhood dream to be a pastor of a large, growing church. I found pastoral work to be fulfilling, my life had purpose and meaning. From a very early age I had enjoyed the admiration and praise of people who looked to me for spiritual leadership and guidance. I felt good about myself. I was a somebody.

Suddenly I was hit by the tidal wave of an unwanted divorce and knocked off the pinnacle of ministerial success. One day I was a somebody. The next day I was, agonizing, a nobody. The people who once looked up to me now looked down at me as if I were forever in their eyes to be a second-class citizen.

Then there were those words in those awful divorce papers that said in effect that I had been a failure as a husband. Worse than that, a complete washout. In my upbringing and background in a conservative church and with my ideals about God's plan and expectation for the family, there's nothing on this earth that could have happened to more shatter my self-image than a divorce.

Day after day, and for many long lonely nights, there didn't seem to be any way to "put Humpty Dumpty back together again." I had fallen off the wall of success with a smashing crash. My once organized, orderly, purposeful life was now like a spool of unraveled yarn all strung out. I didn't see how I could ever get my life back together and feel like a somebody again.

In the large, rambling old house in which I was brought up in Columbus, Ohio, we had a fireplace. It was in the middle of the west wall of our living room. On top of the fireplace, halfway up the wall, perched a magnificent wood mantel. From the mantel to the ceiling, and for approximately five feet across, hung a flawless mirror. There it towered over our entire living room—reflecting, without flaw, any and all images that came through our front door into the living room.

This moment I want you to picture in your mind that beautiful, flawless mirror. See it shining clear and true in its flawless reflection. Do you see it there, in your visualization?

Now, I want you to see a brick suddenly hurled, hitting the mirror dead center, and shattering it into a million pieces. This is a heartbreaking picture that represents many a person's shattered self-esteem. There's nothing like a shattered self-esteem to make you feel like a nobody.

What do you do when you feel like a nobody? Must you drag through life suffering from low self-esteem? How do you recover a lost self-worth? How do you rebuild a shattered self-love?

My heart goes out to every person who feels like a nobody. For whatever reason and however your self-esteem has been shattered, this book is written for you. Let me tell you that no matter what has happened in your life; no matter what you have done wrong; no matter how many times you think you've failed; or no matter how unfairly you think others have treated you, in God's sight you are *not*:

> Broken beyond repair,
> A complete failure,
> A basket case,
> A condemned sinner,
> A forever loser,
> A nobody.

But in God's sight you are a SOMEBODY!

It is the crime of all crimes against yourself to not love yourself as a person of worth and value. This is one crime that never pays. It is the one robbery that no person can afford. Every part of our entire life is either added to or subtracted from by our own self-image, self-image being the way we view and feel about ourself as a person.

Nancy had exceptional talent. People liked her and her family members loved her dearly. Yet, because she did not love herself, she didn't believe anyone else loved her either.

All the time that she was really a somebody, she kept feeling like a nobody. Unbearable feelings of worthlessness drove Nancy to strange and rebellious behavior that brought multiple heartbreak to herself and her family.

People who have a healthy self-love enjoy better health. The word "disease" originally meant not illness but lack of ease. To be ill at ease with oneself promotes disease. A healthy dose of self-love can help prevent heart attacks and many other kinds of illnesses. Studies show that people who have self-love are less accident prone. It's a fact that accepting and developing good feelings about yourself as a person of worth and value is a decisive thing you can do to promote your good health and welfare.

How we feel and think about ourselves effects every relationship of our lives. A low self-image will many times manifest itself by being critical and jealous of the other person's friendships and successes. Inadequate feelings of worth often cause the suffering person who's feeling worthless to throw dirt at another, even though he loses ground himself by doing so. When self-esteem is low, it is most difficult—if not impossible—to accept and love other people. How can we love another person when we don't accept and love ourselves? The answer is, *we can't*.

What is the solution to the problem of low self-esteem? Answering, Jesus lays down this important rule for us to live by: "Thou shalt love the Lord thy God with all thy heart, . . . and thy neighbor as thyself" (Luke 10:27, *KJV*). The way to be a healthy, happy person with meaningful relationships is to practice three interrelated love principles.

Number 1—Love God,
Number 2—Love yourself,
Number 3—Love others.

This commandment to practice three-way love is the heart

and teaching of everything that Jesus said and did. Love begins with God. It is when we accept and receive God's love for us and begin to return that love, that we are able to accept and love ourself as a person of worth and value. The more we practice God's kind of love and give it away to other people, the richer and fuller feelings we enjoy as a person worth loving.

Self-love is the direct opposite of self-centeredness. Self-love frees one from having to think about his miserable self all the time.

UNDERSTAND THESE SIX COMMON CAUSES OF WORTHLESS FEELINGS

The first common cause that makes a person today feel like a nobody is: *The negative society we live in.* Day after day we are hit with the front page of the newspaper that is 97 percent negative. Every time you turn the television on, whether it's a daytime soap opera or the evening newsdowner or the night killing and rape, you stand a better than 90 percent chance that what you see and hear is going to be negative input. Even the weatherman comes on and says, "There is a 10 percent chance of rain today." Why doesn't he say, "There is a 90 percent chance of sunshine."? Because we live in a world that has been spoiled by sin and is negative.

You cannot allow society around you to do your thinking for you. As J.B. Phillips paraphrases Romans 12:2: "Don't let the world squeeze you into its mold." Because if you think like the world around you thinks, you're going to be imprisoned in the negative, and it has been my experience that when I am thinking negatively I always end up feeling crummy about myself. To help you stand out from the crowd and begin to think so you can feel like a somebody, Chapter 6 will show you how to: "Choose a Winning Attitude."

2

The second common cause that makes a person today feel like a nobody is: *Believing the exaggerated things we've been told by other people.* One of the exceptionally attractive single girls who attends our evening Bible fellowship shared this experience. She said that when she was growing up she was convinced that she was the ugliest girl in her class and still suffers feelings that she is not very pretty. She recalled that when she was in the sixth grade the teacher pointed a finger at her and called her "an ugly little girl" in front of all her classmates. How devastating! That one exaggerated, untrue statement had damaged her self-image for all these years. In spite of the fact that she enjoys far more natural beauty than the average woman, she still thinks of herself as being unattractive.

Johnny has trouble in school with reading. The other kids snicker at him. The snickering tells him he is not very bright. Teacher says, "Johnny, I wish you were smart like your older brother that I had." Johnny's mind interprets the comment: I'm dumb. He goes home and Dad says, "You dumb kid, why can't you get reading?" Another seed thought goes in: I'm a dumb kid. Just because Johnny is having trouble reading does not mean that he is a dumb kid. I know a man who is very brilliant. He has a Ph.D. and teaches at a leading university, and he didn't even talk until he was seven years of age. He is anything but a dumb person.

In all of our lives there are things that have been said which are exaggerated untruths or thoughts, and yet we have believed them. One of the things I believed about myself for years was that I could not do anything around the house because I was not a handyman. Somewhere back there, people started feeding that into my computer. I believed it so I helped it along. I always said, "I can't do anything around the house." Pretty good excuse. I accepted it and believed it; therefore I didn't do anything. One of the things I'm finding out, at thirty-eight years of age, is I can hang wallpaper just as well as anyone else.

So, what we need to do is take those exaggerated untruths, examine them, see them for what they are—as falsehoods—and reject them. Get rid of them.

The third common cause that makes a person today feel like a nobody is: *Equating Failure or Failures with Being a Failure.* How far this is from the plain truth. Just because a person has failed the test once or twice, or even three times, does not mean he cannot pass it. It does mean that he is going to have to try harder and put forth greater effort to pass the test. Because you have failed in one job does not mean that you cannot succeed in another. It merely means that you probably weren't suited for that particular job. You are created to do something else, so you find out what it is and you do it. Because you have failed in a marriage or in a friendship does not mean that you cannot improve your ability to get along with another person and have a meaningful, lasting relationship in the future.

There is no one alive who is a complete and final failure. Also, it's true that there is no one but who has failed at something, at some time or other. So stand up and refuse to accept any kind of a failure complex. God never created you to be a failure. God didn't waste His time making nobodys. He spent His very best efforts in creating you to be a learner and an overcomer. Specifically, in chapter 7, I will share with you how to turn your past failures into future blessings.

The fourth common cause that makes a person today feel like a nobody is: *Living Below Our Own Ideals and Standards.* One cannot live like a pig and feel good about it. Neither can one eat garbage and stay healthy in his mind and thoughts. A lot of people are living in strange and promiscuous life-styles and they are reaping the harvest—

feeling terrible about themselves. I know, in my life, when I watch a movie on television which goes against my better judgment and standards, that afterward I always feel degraded and letdown as a person. Often I blame the television station or the network for the crummy movie they've shown, but really it's myself that I am mad at because I've not lived up to my highest ideals. When it comes to feeling good about yourself, it does make a great deal of difference how you live your life.

The fifth common cause that contributes to low self-esteem is: A *Person's Dependency Upon the Wrong Things to Give Him Feelings of Self-Worth.* True self-worth can never be found in either the accumulation of things or in the mad pursuit of doing.

Charles drove himself unsparingly in his work night and day. Year after year he worked seven days a week, ten to fourteen hours, refusing to take much needed vacations. All the while he was neglecting his family. As his children were growing up, he kept telling himself that the long work hours were for their benefit. The unacknowledged truth was that Charles worked those long hours not because his company expected him to; not because his family needed that much money; but because he had an unsatisfied need to feel like a somebody. His unsatisfied need to feel like a worthwhile person drove him to be a workaholic. A driven person is never at peace, nor is he satisfied with himself as a person. When Charles' company went out of business, his whole world fell in on him. And soon the workaholic turned into an alcoholic.

The other day I received a letter from a crushed woman. After telling me about her husband's having one affair after another with a younger woman, she said, "It seems as though I'm not worth loving, even though I try. All my life it's seemed like men have wanted someone else, at least that's how they made me feel.''

In responding back to this brokenhearted woman's cry for help, this is what I said, ''I understand. There isn't anything in this world that hurts any more than to have your mate be unfaithful. It hurts. Oh, how it hurts! But, let me assure you that your worth as a person does not depend on either your sex appeal or your mate's faithfulness to you. I understand that this unfaithfulness batters and bruises your ego. But it does not change God's love for you, nor does it devalue your worth as a precious person in His sight.''

In the chapters to come we are going to learn how you can discover your true worth and come out on top, whether or not you have material things, whether or not you're presently achieving, and regardless of what other people close to you are doing or not doing.

The sixth common cause that makes a person feel like a nobody is: *Playing the Comparison Game*. The comparison game is one that you lose every time, yet how many times we play it! When I compare myself with someone else that I think is better than I am, then I end up feeling like a nobody. On the other hand, when I play the game the other direction and pick out another individual and tear him down to make myself look better than he, I end up feeling crummy for what I've done. So you see, it's true, there is no way to play the comparison game and win. The comparison game only makes us losers. The truth is, as we are going to learn in the next exciting chapter, that you were never created to be compared with another person. You are one of your kind.

HOW DO YOU TELL IF YOU ARE
LACKING IN SELF-ESTEEM

A few months ago when I had selected leaders together for

a training-sharing session, I had them each take a little self-examination test in asking themselves the seven questions that I am going to present to you for your own self-evaluation. Without exception, everyone of the people present came up lacking in having a sufficient supply of self-worth. Here are the questions to determine if you also lack in this all-vital area of self-worth.

1. *Are you considered overly sensitive by friends or family?* All of us have our feelings hurt at some time. None of us are immune to rejection or insult. The acid test is: Are you more easily offended than most people? Does it require a long time for you to recover from a hurt?

2. *Are you argumentative?* Some people feel an overwhelming urge to argue. They have an excessive need to prove their point; they have to prove who's right, who's wrong. Or, can you allow other people to have a viewpoint that differs from yours and still be friends?

3. *Are you a critical person?* An excessively critical attitude is a dead giveaway. It reveals an individual who has a very poor opinion of himself. The worst critic is usually the one who is the most unhappy himself. He dislikes himself intensely and when he gets fed up with his own self-hate, he takes it out in the form of criticism of others. Question: Do you have to tear others down to build yourself up?

4. *Are you forgiving?* Those who lack a proper amount of self-love hold on to misdeeds of the past, they are the grudge-holders and find it very difficult to forgive. The unforgiving person does irreparable harm to his personality. To cling to an unforgiving spirit is a terrible thing to do to yourself. In Matthew, in the Sermon on the Mount, Jesus made it clear that an unforgiving spirit blocks the flow of God's blessing—spiritually and emotionally—into our lives.

5. *Are you excessively jealous?* Love yourself—or else succumb to jealousy. Shakespeare called jealousy "the green-eyed monster." The Bible calls it sin. Do you rejoice when other people get the promotion? Do you help other people to fulfill their dreams? Or do you have to say something degrading about the other person who is achieving? It is our own feeling of worthlessness or low achievement that makes us jealous of another person.

6. *Are you a poor listener?* I once had a friend who enjoyed telling endless stories and jokes. When he was talking his eyes sparkled, but I noticed that when other people were talking he never listened. Such a person is so preoccupied with his own feelings and his own importance, he cannot bring himself to listen to anyone. A healthy dose of self-love frees one to really be interested in others.

7. *Do you find it hard to accept compliments?* Lacking in self-love, some people respond to a compliment by saying, "Oh, I thought what I did was awful." Or, they go the other extreme and respond, "Yes, I agree, it was pretty wonderful." When we don't think much of ourself, it is very difficult to accept praise and words of appreciation. The right response to a compliment is a simple and kind "thank you" and smile. That kind of response lifts both you and the giver to a place of warmth and friendship.

Well, how did you come out in the self-esteem personal evaluation test? If you are lacking in self-esteem, then be assured you are a member of the majority party. When it comes to self-esteem, just about everyone I know has a need for growth and improvement. Do yourself a big favor and admit your need for more self-love.

There is a large dose of self-love for what ails you awaiting you in the chapters that follow. It's yours for the reading and application. But first, to benefit the most from it you must honestly admit to yourself your need for more self-love. There is no emotional or spiritual growth without taking the first step of admitting a personal need for it. What can happen to the individual who opens up to God, to experience either a birth or renewal of self-love and worth, is absolutely fantastic.

COMMIT YOURSELF TO DO WHATEVER IT TAKES TO HAVE BETTER FEELINGS ABOUT YOURSELF. To have better feelings about yourself is worth whatever effort it might take on your part. I believe that God wants you to experience self-approval, self-acceptance, self-esteem and to love yourself, even as He loves you. This is the miracle that God wants to work within every one of us, to transform "a nobody" into a "somebody."

Someone asked a veteran farmer why his harvest was so great and he replied, "It is a miracle of God. But, first I had to plant it, fertilize it regularly, water daily, and put forth my best efforts." You make the commitment to do whatever it takes to have good feelings about yourself, as you read the coming chapter, and I believe that God will give you the desire of your heart.

A richer self-esteem is waiting for you.
A new you is about to be born.
So let's move ahead
to improve the way we think
and feel about ourselves.

2

❧✦❧

Make the Wonderful Discovery of Your Tremendous Worth

2

On a Friday afternoon a sixth grade teacher said to her pupils, "This week we have been studying the subject of self-esteem. Today we are going to have a little oral review on what we have learned." With that introduction, she turned to Philip, a Spanish-American who lived in the poor section of their small town with his parents who were migrant farm workers. She asked, "Philip, do you understand what self-esteem means?" Feeling good at having been chosen, anxiously he replies, "Yes, ma'am. It means that even though I come from a poor family I'm still a somebody because God made me someone special."

I wish everyone had Philip's understanding about their own worth as a person. How fortunate is the person who enjoys good healthy feelings of self-worth. The other day, a middle-aged man whose luck had really been down, who is convinced his mother never wanted him, and who has been jobless for a long time, said to me, "I'd give anything if I just felt like I had some worth in this world." You don't have to have been an unloved and unwanted child to feel worthless. Neither do you have to be without a job to feel worthless. One of the tragedies of our time is that so many people have lost sight of their own beauty and worth as a person. To say you are worthless is to falsify the truth.

This very day I want you to make the wonderful discovery of your own tremendous worth and value as a person. No matter how worthless you might feel; no matter what limitations you think you have; no matter what has happened in your life; no matter who doesn't love you; no matter how inferior to someone else you might feel, you are *not:*

An ugly person,
A born loser,
A complete failure,
A person without value.

To God you are:

More majestic than a mountain,
More vast and complex than the ocean,
More wise than an owl or any other
    living being.
More beautiful than a sunset.
More lovable than a teddy bear.

WORTH MORE THAN ALL GOD'S WONDERFUL CREATON—THAT'S YOU

What a CREATOR God is! ''The heavens declare the glory of God; and the firmament showeth his handiwork'' (Psalm 19:1, *KJV*).

Get away from it all, take a walk in the woods, hike in the mountains, stroll along the beach. Open your eyes and you will see how perfectly and masterfully every detail of nature has been designed by the Master Designer.

But of all God's marvelous creations, you are His greatest! You are the finest, the choice, and the best! Of all others, you alone are created in His perfect image, after the likeness of God Himself. To you He has given the mental facility called the brain, weighing less than ten pounds, yet with the ability to assimilate more data than could be stored in the Empire State Building using the most complex computers. You are really something! Not only can you think by assimilating and making decisions, but you can feel every emotion in existence through your fantastic nerve network system. Add to all this your ability to communicate with others and even with God Himself.

My friend you are wonderfully made! God has made you only "a little lower than the angels, and (has) crowned (you) with glory and honor" (Psalm 8:5, *KJV*). He made you "to have dominion over the works of (His) hands . . ." (Psalm 8:6, *KJV*). What should be our response to how wonderfully God has made us? Make this response your response: "I will praise God; for I am wonderfully made" (see Psalm 139:14).

GOD DIDN'T CREATE YOU TO BE A NOBODY BUT A SOMEBODY

As Ethel Waters so affectionately says, "God didn't sponsor no flops." God created you with tremendous worth. A while back, in Chicago, Illinois, a woman was granted a million dollars because she had lost her eyesight in an accident. I want to ask you a question. Which one of you would trade places with that woman? Would you trade your eyesight for one million dollars? I, for one, certainly would not. I heard about a young teenage boy who was the victim of a diving accident in a public swimming pool in which his neck was broken and he was paralyzed from the waist down. It has been reported that he received close to a million dollars in his suit against the pool owners. The only problem is, he must spend the rest of his life confined to a wheelchair. Would you take a million dollars and sit in a wheel chair the rest of your life? You might be tempted to, but one thing is for sure—after the first week you would be glad to give the money back and get out of the wheelchair. Already, with the use of your eyesight and with the use of your legs, you are worth two million dollars. Add up your brain, the hundreds of working parts in your physical body, your emotions that give you the ability to feel, and you are worth millions of dollars. You see, as God made you, you are already a millionaire.

While Jesus was here on earth, unveiling to us some of the hidden treasures of life, He taught that the eternal soul was worth more than the entire universe when He said, "For what shall it profit a man, if he shall gain the whole world, and lose his own soul" (Mark 8:36, *KJV*). If you were to take all the sparkling diamonds in the world, all the shining gold, and all the silver and stack all of the world's most treasured valuables together in one pile—you, my friend, according to Jesus, are worth more than all of this. In God's sight you are worth more than all these things that people treasure most.

CREATED TO BE A SOMEBODY SPECIAL—THAT'S YOU

Not only will you never find two snowflakes exactly alike; not only will you never find two pebbles on the beach that are the same; not only will you never find two blades of grass that are identical; but genetic scientists have said that if you had three hundred billion brothers and sisters, none of them would be exactly like you. There is no one who has ever lived before or now who is your exact equal. *You are a divine original.*

You are not a pale copy of an original, but you are the original creation of yourself. Originals are always worth more than the copies. It has been reported that one of Rembrandt's paintings sold for over one million dollars. Why did it sell for one million dollars? First of all, it had been painted by the master of painters. Secondly, because it was an original painting. Thirdly, because there were no more like it anywhere in the world. My friend, you are not here on this earth by chance, but you were planned for and created by the Master Himself. As God made you, there is no one else just like you. You are a divine original—a person who is unique, distinct and special.

Jokingly someone said, "It's a good thing that God created man. If man had made man, we probably would have all been standardized types run off a vast assembly line with no individual uniqueness." God in his greatness made us with many likenesses, yet each as an individual of distinction.

LOVED BY GOD—THAT'S YOU!

God thinks you are worth loving. If you have been thinking that you are not worth loving, then you need to change the way you think. To think of yourself as anything other than a worthwhile person is to think wrong. Some of you have been thinking wrongly about yourself, not just this week or last week, or this year, but throughout your entire lifetime. In your mind there has been formed the habit of putting yourself down. This degrading way of thinking is self-defeating. It is one of the results of sin in our world and lives. I believe in the power of God not only to transform a person's heart, but to change the way he thinks. Not only does God want to forgive us of our sins, to set us free to live clean in an unclean world, but he wants to change our destructive thought habits into constructive ones. It is so important how we think about ourselves because, as the Bible says, "As he (a man) thinketh in his heart, so is he . . ." (Proverbs 23:7, *KJV*).

One of my favorite stories is about a boy who made his own little boat out of wood. After he had worked for days and long hours shaping it and forming it, he held it up and said, "It's mine, I made it." The next day with exhuberant anticipation, he carried his boat to the shore of the lake and sailed it on the clear, blue water. The little boat that was his pride and joy skipped along as the gentle breezes blew its sails across the rippling waves. Then unexpectedly, suddenly, a gust of wind caught the little boat snapping the string the boy held it by. Out further and further the little boat sailed until the heartbroken little boy, straining his eyes, could see it no more. Crestfallen, the little boy made his way home—without his boat. That which he had made was gone.

The weeks and months went by. Then one day as the boy passed a toy shop, something caught his full attention. Could it be? Was it really? He looked closer. It was! Yes, there it was in the display window. Sure enough, there was his own little boat. Overwhelmed with joy, the boy dashed into the store to claim his possession. Excitedly he told the owner that was his boat on display. It really did belong to him. He had made it with his own hands, hadn't he? "I'm sorry," the storekeeper said, "but it's my boat now. If you want it, you will have to pay the price for it."

Disappointed once again, the boy left the store. But he was determined to get his boat back, even though it meant working hard and saving everything he could make until he had enough money to buy his boat back.

At last the day came. Tightly holding his money in his fist, he proudly walked into the shop, spread his hard-earned money on the counter top and said, "I've come to buy my boat back." The clerk counted the money. It was the exact amount. Reaching into the showcase, the storekeeper took the boat and handed it to the eager boy. The lad's face lit up with a smile of satisfaction as he held the little boat in his arms. "You're mine," he said, "twice mine. Mine because I made you, and now mine because I paid the price to buy you back."

Not only did God make you special in the beginning, but when you were lost and drifting away from your Maker, He paid the ransom price in sending His Son, Jesus Christ, to die for your sins to buy you back. It is apart from God that man loses his worth and value, while it is back in fellowship with God that man's true worth is restored. The question is, why did God give everything He had to buy you back? It is because God loves you. God not only sees our sins but He sees beyond that to our worth and our unlimited potential as He first made us.

God believes you are worth loving

You mean, even with my sins? Yes.
Even with that which is degrading to
    look at about myself? Yes.
Even with my faults? Yes.
Even with my shameful past? Yes.
Even with all my failures? Yes.
Even with all my rebellion? Yes.
Even with all my faults and imperfections? Yes.

If you were the only
sinner in the world,
God loves you so much,
Jesus would have died
to restore your lost dignity! [1]

God sent Jesus Christ to die on a cross to eliminate the bad, the degrading, the defeating, the shameful—our sins, and to bring out the best in us. *God believes in you. Now start believing in Him that you might believe in yourself.* Jesus Christ died to restore your lost self-respect. To give you back your lost dignity. To make you able to walk with your head up high. God loves you as if you were the only one in this world to love. Wow! What a great love God has for

---

1. Dale E. Galloway, *You Can Win with Love,* (Irvine, CA: Harvest House Publishers, 1976), p. 53.

you. God loves you—that is a fact. And who are you—to not love what God loves?

TO REALIZE AND ACTUALIZE YOUR TREMENDOUS WORTH AS A PERSON TAKE THESE NINE STEPS

1. *Claim your sonship.* "But as many as received him, to them gave he power to become the sons of God, even to them that believe on his name" (John 1:12, *KJV*). Sonship is God's intent and plan for you. It is your birthright. "See how very much our heavenly Father loves us, for he allows us to be called his children—think of it—and we really are!" (1 John 3:1, *TLB*).

A woman about to give up on her marriage came to see me. All the time that she talked, she kept looking down. As she described her drug addict husband's abuse and mistreatment, I saw her as suffering something worse than physical abuse. She was beaten in her own self-esteem. Worthless and inferior feelings dominated her life. Openly she shared her hunger to know Jesus personally and ended by admitting she didn't know how. What a privilege it was for me to lead her, word by word, in a prayer of committment to Jesus. Having claimed her sonship for the first time, I saw a smile break across her face. Then I noticed the droop in her shoulders was gone. By receiving Jesus as Lord, (and that makes you feel worth something) a whole new life came to my new friend. That day worth replaced worthlessness. Yes, Jesus put worth into our lives.

2. *Accept yourself as a person that God loves.* We were standing in a prayer circle, under the fir trees, at our Spring retreat. First there had been a number of one-sentence prayers of thanksgiving to the Lord. Then we started praying in love, one for the other, and suddenly we were bathing in the warm love of Christ's presence. One of our prayer partners was a man in his late twenties, who grew up feeling

putdown and unloved by his parents. At an early age he had gotten in trouble with both the school authorities and with the law; he had already been through one marriage, and was now into destructive fighting in the present marriage. A few months earlier, this young man had become a Christian which had begun so many wondrous changes in his life. That day in our prayer circle, while enjoying close fellowship, my friend was hit with the impact of God's love for him. And in response, with healing tears streaming down his face, he looked up into the heavens and said, "Thank you, God, for loving me as I am. I actually believe now, for the first time in my life, that because you love me, I can love myself." Since that holy moment of acceptance neither my friend nor his family have been without love!

To you, God says,

> My child,
>> I love you.
> My child,
>> I accept you.
> My child,
>> I care about you.
> My child,
>> I forgive you.
> My child,
>> I am going to use you.
> My child,
>> I am with you all the
>> way.

So now—Accept God's love and love yourself.

God accepts us right where we are. The minute we receive Jesus as Lord, He gives us the name Christian and says, "Let's go together from here and I will help you grow into that name." God accepts you, now accept yourself. Look beyond your sin, your faults, your failures, what's wrong with you, and see what is right. Basically you are a good person who needs some more improvement. When we are living in fellowship with God, then we have the promise that we stand as perfect in God's eyes because Jesus takes up the slack. "But if we are living in the light of God's presence, just as Christ does, then we have wonderful fellowship and joy with each other, and the blood of Jesus his Son cleanses us from every sin" (1 John 1:7, *TLB*). Now, give yourself the smile of approval that you need.

3. *Get a clear picture of your own abilities.* There is an old saying, "Know yourself." The Bible says it this way, "Be honest in your estimate of yourselves, measuring your value by how much faith God has given you" (Romans 12:3, *TLB*). What a waste to downgrade one's own abilities. To say, "I can't do that," when you know good and well that you can. It must grieve God to see people waste and wail away their days in self-pity. To not accept, develop, and use the abilities and gifts that God has given to you is to commit the sin of ingratitude.

On the other hand, to over-sell yourself and to think that you can do anything without other people and without God is to get too big for your britches. A man that has come to an honest view of himself does not have to toot his own horn or to show off what he has or hasn't got. A man that has forgotten who his source is, who has forgotten from where his value and worth comes, is headed for a letdown.

What then is a sane and proper view of oneself? It is the view of seeing yourself as a person who can do things, but not everything—a person that has value and worth, who is dependent upon God for his strength and help. I have found that ". . . my help cometh from the Lord." It is in Him that life takes on true value and begins to realize its full potential.

Without Him my value deflates like a tire with a hole in it.

4. *Put perfectionism down.* Let me ask you a question: How many perfect people are there in the world? Let's ask it another way: What Christian do you know who lives a perfect Christian life in both attitude and actions? Do you know what? If you expect me to be perfect or anyone else to be perfect, you are going to be disillusioned. If you expect perfect performance out of yourself, you are going to be defeated constantly. The apostle Paul confessed his own imperfection when he said, "I don't mean to say I am perfect. I haven't learned all I should . . ." (Philippians 3:12, *TLB*). The man who wrote thirteen of twenty-seven books in our New Testament saw himself as in the process of learning how to live God's way. Don't forget you are a learner. Don't forget I'm a learner. We are all learning together. Take comfort in these words, made famous by Bill Gothard: "God is not finished with me yet."

5. *Accept anything that is unchangeable about your physical appearance.* Just about everyone has something about their physical appearance they would like to change. Change what you can. Improve where you can improve. Dress up what you can dress up to make you feel better about yourself. On the other hand, why be defeated about what you can't change. There are some things you cannot change. You can change your weight, but you can't change your height.

In my early teens, about the time I started to notice there were girls, my hair began to curl. Ever since I have had curly, kinky hair. For years, I've tried a variety of hairdos to straighten out the curls. In the past I have spent hours blowing my hair dry, attempting to take out the curls. Finally I've come to the point of accepting the fact that I have curly hair. So now, instead of wanting to be like another man who has straight hair, I've decided to be myself, and wear my hair naturally curly like it is. It's a good feeling to accept yourself as you are. You don't have to be taller or shorter to be an acceptable person. You don't have to look like someone else looks to be a beautiful you. It is unbelievable what physical characteristics we zero in on, and make mountains out of mole hills.

Whatever it is that bothers you about your own physical appearance, I'm going to tell you how to be free from it. I know that some people are changed physically through plastic surgery. May I suggest you have spiritual surgery? Cup in your hands whatever it is that you find unacceptable about your appearance. Cup your hands together and put in the wart, the baldness, the being too short, the flat chest, whatever it is that bothers you. Now, lift your cupped hands up as high as you can. Let go of it, and give it to God. As you let go of it, in prayer commit it to God. Turn your hands over, spread your fingers clear apart and let go of it. Now bow your head and thank God for the physical beauty of make-up that you do have.

Center on the positive appearance that you do have. Give God the negative that you don't like, and be set free to give yourself the smile of approval.

6. *Forgive and forget your strikeouts.* Someone has said, "The man that makes no mistakes does not usually make anything." If you attempt to achieve anything worthwhile in life, you can expect some failings and some setbacks. Do you know that Babe Ruth not only was the home run king but he holds the record for the number of strikeouts in a season? Suppose Ruth would have centered on his striking out, condemned himself as being a hopeless hitter. This would have destroyed his confidence. He would have stopped going to the plate and swinging. The world never would have had a baseball home run king by the name of Babe Ruth. When you strike out, forgive and forget. Get back in there and start swinging again.

See your failings or weaknesses as opportunities to draw close to God. Once again the apostle Paul discovered this wonderful truth. He writes: "I am quite happy about 'the thorn,' and about the insults and hardships, persecutions and difficulties; for when I am weak, then I am strong,—the less I have, the more I depend on him" (2 Corinthians 12:10, *TLB*).

7. *Believe this wonderful truth: You are not inferior to anyone.* Different, yes, wonderfully different! Wouldn't it be a dull world if we were all alike? Never forget you are God's idea—and God only dreams up fantastic ideas. No other person has the same God-given potential, the identical cluster of spiritual gifts, and the exact same abilities that you have. So, accept yourself and stop wishing you were a different person.

8. *Begin now and forever to refuse to play the destructive comparison game.* To play the deadly comparison game is to engage in self-devaluating behavior. Every time we play the game the bottom drops out of our feeling of self-worth. Just the other day I came home to find my lovely, usually self-confident wife, Margi, lamenting the fact that she didn't look like the models pictured in the popular cosmetic magazine she had been looking through. Coming off a bout with the flu, she didn't feel all that good about her appearance to begin with. To me, if ever there was a real beauty, it's my wife, Margi. Yet, the old comparison game had put her on a real downer.

From firsthand experience let me tell you that playing the comparison game is always an emotional downer. It opens the door to doubting one's own worth as a person, and it breeds self-pity and contempt for oneself. Every time I go to a book store, if I don't discipline myself, before I know it I am comparing myself to some other writer and undercutting my own work as an author. Playing the comparison game has yet to have done me, you, or anyone else any good. So why play this destructive game?

9.   *Daily affirm your own worth by making these affirmations (say them out loud):*

> Of all God's wondrous creation—
> > I am His greatest!
> Created to be someone special—
> > That's me!
> Jesus died for me because
> > He believed I was worth loving.
> Because God so loves me—
> > I am going to love myself.
> What could be greater than
> > to be a child of God?
> Yes, I do have imperfections—
> > but God is not finished with me yet.
> "I can do all things through
> > Christ which strengtheneth me." [2]
> With Christ's help, I will
> > refuse to play the comparison game
> > and I will develop my own God-given
> > potential by helping other people.

Make these self-esteem building affirmations yours. Say them repeatedly—morning, noon, night and in between—until the truth of your self-worth sinks into your subconscious mind. Do these things we have learned together in this chapter and believe me:

> YOU WILL MAKE
> THE WONDERFUL DISCOVERY
> OF
> YOUR TREMENDOUS WORTH.

2. Philippians 4:13, *KJV.*

3

Get a Fresh New Start

3

❦

At some time or other, just about everyone needs a fresh new start. Things happen, mistakes are made, dreams are dashed, and the taste of life turns sour.

Do you need a fresh new start? A lot of people do. Almost every day I talk to someone who for one reason or another needs a new start. Possibly:

> You are without a job.
> You have just been devastated by divorce.
> You are at loss from the death of your mate.
> Your marriage is on a rocky road.
> Your financial problems are mounting.
> You feel like you've been a failure.
> Your life has been going from bad to worse.
> You long for some new purpose in life.
> You want something more out of life.

It is true that for many of us life would become unbearable if it were not for the opportunity for a fresh new beginning. God's word is: WE CAN START AGAIN. As my friend, Stanly Baldwin, says in his book, *What Makes You So Special*: "He even designed nature to give us 365 brand new days every year, 365 fresh new starts, 365 occasions to put yesterdays behind us."[3] *God made everyday to be a new day.*

3. Stanley C. Baldwin, *What Makes You So Special?* (Grand Rapids, MI: Baker Book House Company, 1977), p. 5.

Malcolm was hurting so deeply emotionally that he couldn't speak three words without sobbing. A gentle man, in his early 40's, he had just been forsaken by his wife who had gotten turned on to another lover. Out of the anguish of a breaking heart he asked, "Pastor, is life over for me?" When life tumbles in, your back is against the wall, when everything looks dark, the question is: Is there any hope?

WHATEVER HAPPENS—NEVER GIVE UP HOPE!

About now your're thinking, "Yeh, it's easy for you to tell me to never give up hope, but what do you know about having everything go wrong in your life?"

Let me tell you, I know what it is to hurt. I know what it is to feel like your life is over. Seven years ago everything that meant anything to me in my life tumbled in on top of me. At age 31, climbing the peaks of ministerial success, both my family life and my professional life were smashed by an unwanted divorce. To a pastor like myself, nothing could have been a more unacceptable failure than what was happening in my life. Divorce meant that I had failed miserably. I would lose my wife, my two children that I loved and adored and who now live 2500 miles away from me. My ministerial career that had been my lifetime pursuit and desire was ruined. Many good Christian people whom I respected pronounced the sentence of doom upon me as being finished in the ministry. They looked upon me as so much debri from another shipwreck in the sea of life.

At this point of brokenness, confusion and total darkness, for the first time in my life the will to die was stronger than the will to live. No one but God and me will ever know how close I came to giving up all hope, to giving up my faith in God. Faith in God is hope. Without faith in God when reverses happen in our lives, there is no hope of a better tomorrow. But whatever has happened to you, whatever you do—*Don't ever give up hope.*

Without hope, a person quits trying. I like the story of the little boy who came home his first day of school and made this startling announcement to his father. He said, "Dad, I quit!" His Dad said, "What do you mean? One day in school and you quit?" The little boy replied, "I can't read, I can't write, and the teacher won't let me talk. What's the use? I quit!" There is one thing for sure—when you give up, things are not going to get any better. It is that stubborn hope that reaches out for a better tomorrow.

GOD SPECIALIZES IN NEW BEGINNINGS

The wonder of creation tells us that—
    God specializes in new beginnings.
The cry of a newborn babe tells us that—
    God specializes in new beginnings.
The flowers breaking into bloom with the new Spring
    tells us—God specializes in new beginnings.
The sun rising over the distant mountainpeak
    Announcing the arrival of a new day tells us—
    God specializes in new beginnings.

God sent His son, Jesus, to this earth to give us a new start. Jesus didn't come to help those who are perfect. He came, giving himself as a ransom to save sinners. Jesus is the HELPER of those who need help. At the very beginning of his public ministry He stood at the front of the synagogue and spoke these most meaningful words: "The Spirit of the Lord is upon me; he has appointed me to preach Good News to the poor; he has sent me to heal the brokenhearted and to announce that captives shall be released and the blind shall see, that the downtrodden shall be freed from their oppressors, and that God is ready to give blessings to all who come to him" (Luke 4:18, 19, *TLB*).

I know from firsthand experience that failure is a heavy

Don't stick to your failing behavior.
Do something to change, improve, make it work again!

load to carry. There are many negative thinking people who would try to make us believe that once a person has failed, he is forever branded a second-class person at best. Nothing could be more foreign to the gospel that Jesus preached and bought with His death. To all of you, who are in some way bruised, bleeding, or broken, Jesus speaks these words: "Come unto me, all ye that labor and are heavy laden, and I will give you rest" (Matthew 11:28, *KJV*).

Possibly you have lost hope. I don't think there is anything worse than to lose hope. As Jesus was arrested, accused and crucified, the disciples lost all hope. Their dreams were dashed, it seemed their lives were smashed in a million pieces and they couldn't see anything but darkness. They were afraid and they were in despair as they sat behind closed doors, hiding. Then it happened.

"But on the first day of the week, at early dawn, they came to the tomb, bringing the spices which they had prepared. And they found the stone rolled away from the tomb, but when they entered, they did not find the body of the Lord Jesus. And it happened that while they were perplexed about this, behold, two men suddenly stood near them in dazzling apparel; and as the women were terrified and bowed their faces to the ground, the men said to them, 'Why do you seek the living One among the dead? He is not here, but He has risen. Remember how He spoke to you while He was still in Galilee, saying that the Son of Man must be delivered into the hands of sinful men, and be crucified, and the third day rise again'" (Luke 24: 1-7, *NASB*).

THEY CAME WITHOUT HOPE
BUT LEFT WITH THE GREATEST OF HOPE.

찬'능 5 35
" 어두움속에 "

Yes, sooner or later there comes into every life a long, dark night. You feel like all is lost. You wonder how you can go on.

But because Jesus lives—there is hope that:

After the night comes a new day.
After the storm comes the sun breaking through.
After the winter comes a new spring.
After sin comes forgiveness.
After hurt comes healing.
After setback comes a new advance.
After loss and pain comes gain.
After despair comes new hope.
After sadness comes new joy.
After defeat comes victory.
After death comes the resurrection.

아침에는 기쁨이 오리로다.

Ψ 30 = 5

Yes, it's true, *JOY COMETH IN THE MORNING!*

I like the story that Dr. Charles Allen, one of my favorite writers, relates. A little girl asked her father the question, "What was God doing last night during the storm?" Before he could answer, she answered her own question: "I know," she said excitedly, "God was making the morning." So it is with the storms that come in our lives. All the while that—to us—it looks so dark and we are afraid; God is at work making mornings. *After the night comes the morning.*

The resurrection of Jesus from the dead tells us that God specializes in new beginnings. The resurrection means that a new life for whosoever will come to the Lord Jesus has begun—a life of overcoming anything and everything that defeats us.

BECAUSE JESUS LIVES
FOR YOU—A NEW DAY IS DAWNING

Jesus wants to give you a brand new beginning. He is the

One that makes all things new. When others thought my ministerial life was over (and, to me, if that was over, my life was over), I looked to Jesus and asked Him to give me a new beginning. To Him I gave my sins, my failures, my ill feelings, my hurts, my reputation and my broken dreams; and I believed that out of everything that was wrong, He would bring something good. Thank the Lord I do not live anymore in despair, in self-pity, or in the brokenness of the past. To me God has given a new love to cherish; two more children to love; a new dream to fulfill; new friends to share life with; and a new ministry of new hope to scores of people.

This very day Jesus lives. He is alive. He is present and ready to help you right where you are. Reach out in a simple prayer to Jesus. Feel Him now take your hand. With Christ's steady hand and power at work within your life, you too can turn your:

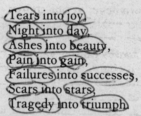

Tears into joy,
Night into day,
Ashes into beauty,
Pain into gain,
Failures into successes,
Scars into stars,
Tragedy into triumph

TO GET A FRESH NEW START—DO THESE EIGHT THINGS

1. *Be born again.* To be born again means to become a brand new person. Being born again is no ordinary, everyday happening. When it happens to you, it is one unforgettable experience! It is so life-changing, and so all comprehensive that no atomic bomb can compare to its powerful changing effect in human life. What all the psychiatrists, doctors, teachers, counselors and agencies that work with people

cannot do to change the human being, Jesus does in the twinkling of an eye.

Being born spritually is such a magnificent miracle that changes an individual from the inside-out, that every time it happens I get all excited and stand amazed at the power of God. Only God can

—take a messed up life and straighten it out.
—turn a hateful heart into a loving heart.
—change a depressed wife into a joyful wife.
—convert an indifferent, selfish husband into an attentive, considerate husband.
—set an enslaved drug addict free,
—give purpose to a bored and meaningless life.
—wipe clean all our sin and guilt.
—transform someone with a poor, miserable self-image into a worthwhile child of God.

It has been our privilege, at our church, to hear firsthand about one of the most publicized conversions of this century. Charles Colson was our guest and gave his personal testimony. When Charles Colson was with us he shared how he was known as Richard Nixon's political hatchet man, and how he sat in the inner circle of Nixon men that held the power of the world in their hands. Yet, in the midst of all this worldly success that Charles Colson had achieved, worked for, clawed for, did almost anything to get—there was within him a discontent—an unquenchable desire for something more in life.

The fall from power of the Nixon men only added disillusionment to Charles Colson's discontent. Wondrously and wonderfully, God used the shining light of a Christian friend to show Charles Colson a better way.

Then, early on a Friday morning while sitting alone staring at the sea, Colson—who had never gone to church before but had seen Jesus in his Christian friends—spoke these simple words of commitment from his heart, "Lord Jesus, I believe you. I accept you. Please come into my life. I am committed to you." Said Charles Colson, "With these words that morning, while the sea churned, came a sureness of mind that matched the depth of feeling in my heart. There something more: strength and serenity, a wonderful new assurance about life, a fresh perception of myself and the world around me. In the process, I felt old fears, tensions and animosities drain away. I was coming alive to things I had never seen before: as if God was filling the barren void that I had known for so many years, filling it to its brim with a whole new kind of awareness."[4] This born again experience, this work of God, changed a political hatchet man into a child of God to be used in the ministry to men in prison.

If God can change Charles Colson and make him a new person, if God can so change a man filled with hate as Eldridge Cleaver was, into a gentle person through which the love of God flows so beautifully, He can change you. The miracle of new birth is for you: "If any man be in Christ, he is a new creature: old things are passed away; behold, all things are become new" (2 Corinthians 5:17, *KJV*).

HOW CAN A MAN BE BORN AGAIN?

"Born again!" exclaimed Nicodemus. "What do you mean? How can an old man go back into his mother's womb and be born again?" (John 3:4, *TLB*). Jesus replies to Nicodemus by explaining that men can only reproduce human life, but that it is the Holy Spirit who initiates and gives this new life that comes from Heaven. It is a mystery and work of God in the human heart.

4. Charles Colson, *Born Again* (Old Tappan, N. J.: Fleming H. Revell, 1976), 130.

WHO CAN BE BORN AGAIN? "For God so loved the world, that . . . whosoever believeth in him should not perish . . ." (John 3:16, *KJV*). Anyone who will do these four things right now, can be born again. Here are the A, B, C, D's of what you must do to be born again.

ADMIT YOU ARE A SINNER. There are a lot of people who will never get into the Kingdom of God, tragically so, because they are too caught up in self-deception to admit their own sins. All have sinned. But only the man who says "I am a sinner" and cries for mercy will find forgiveness.

BELIEVE ON THE LORD JESUS CHRIST AND YOU SHALL BE SAVED. Some years ago there was a man who was going to push a wheelbarrow across Niagara Falls on a tightrope. He was a real promoter so there was a lot of publicity, and on the day he was to perform this stunt a large crowd gathered at the sight of the Falls. The stunt man got on the public address system and pumped up the crowd's enthusiasm; then he concluded by asking, "Do all of you believe that I can do this? If you believe it, raise your hands." The crowd all raised their hands. Why not, they didn't have anything to lose. At that moment, the stunt man zeroed in on a young man who was enthusiastically waving his hand in the air and directed the question right at him: "Do *you* believe that I can push this wheelbarrow across the Falls on that tightrope?" The stuntman said, "Great! You're just the man I'm looking for to ride across in the wheelbarrow." Do you know what? The young man would not get in the wheelbarrow.

You don't really believe in Jesus until you get up and get in the wheelbarrow. Everyone that came to Jesus, Jesus asked to take an action step of faith. Now, let go of yourself and pray the prayer to Jesus.

CONFESS AND REPENT OF YOUR SINS. When I was a

young boy I used to do a lot of confessing of my sins before I got in bed at night to ease my conscience a little bit. But, the next day I would live the same way. To repent means to be so sorry for your sins, that you forsake them; you don't want anything more to do with them. The only way to enter the Kingdom is by confession and repentance. Jesus said, "The Kingdom of God is at hand; repent and believe in the gospel" (Mark 1:15, *NASB*).

DENY YOURSELF. Jesus said, "If anyone wishes to come after Me, let him deny himself, and take up his cross, and follow Me" (Mark 8:34, *NASB*). What does that mean? That means that you stop running your own life and turn the controls over to Jesus. You make the commitment right now that from this minute forward you will live life exactly the way Jesus wants you to live.

You need a new direction in your life,
You need a new life-style,
You need a purpose for living,
You need a new start,
THEN—

LET JESUS CHRIST
COME INTO YOUR HEART.

2. *Accept God's forgiveness.* The Bible tells us that, "If we confess our sins, he is faithful and just to forgive us . . ." (1 John 1:9, *KJV*). In the Old Testament we are promised that when we confess our sins God takes them and casts them as far as the east is from the west and remembers them against us no more.

The second step in accepting God's forgiveness is to accept and forgive yourself. This is so important that I am devoting the entire next chapter to this under the title, "Stop All Self-Condemnation." The truth is, we don't really completely accept God's forgiveness until we stop torturing ourselves with self-blame and forgive ourselves.

3. *Freely forgive others*. Do you know that the only way you can have a continuing relationship with any other person is to practice forgiveness. For example, if you and I became friends and you knew me well enough and long enough, I can guarantee you that there would be something you'd need to forgive me for if we were to have a continuing relationship. The very fact that every person is imperfect in his actions and attitudes, and makes mistakes, tells us that to demand perfection out of another person is to ask for the impossible.

Failing to forgive strains and destroys relationships. A middle-aged man asked me why a woman's memory was as long as an elephant's trunk. When I asked him what he meant he said, "My wife remembers in minute detail every thing I did wrong twenty years ago." With pain showing through on his face he said, "Why can't she forget?" Then he added, "If only she would forget and forgive, we could begin fresh to fall in love again instead of existing in this horrible stalemate."

How foolish it is to destroy the beauty of what could be today because of holding on to what was done wrong yesterday. Forgiveness is the one saving Grace that can set you free to begin again. A person is never wiser or does any human become more divine than the moment he forgives another. "Your heavenly Father will forgive you if you forgive those who sin against you; but if you refuse to forgive them, he will not forgive you" (Matthew 6:14, *TLB*.).

4. *Learn all you can from your mistakes*. What is the most important thing you can do with your past mistakes? There are two kinds of people, those who learn from their mistakes and those who don't. The very best thing you can do is to, with Jesus' help, learn all you can from your mistakes. Learn

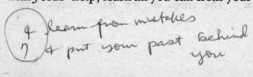

what pitfalls to avoid. Learn where it is you need to improve.

I found it helps tremendously to accept God's unconditional love. How freeing it is to realize that He loves us in spite of the mistakes we have made. The acceptance of God's love gives me the courage to look at myself honestly and admit to what it is that I need to work on.

See failings as opportunities for you to learn. Opportunities to learn how to do things better the next time. I personally have learned so much more from my failings than I have from my successes. Think on this verse from Scripture: "A man who refuses to admit his mistakes can never be successful. But if he confesses and forsakes them, he gets another chance" (Proverbs 28:13, *TLB*).

5. *Turn your weakness into your strong point.* Some people saddle themselves with self-defeating limitations. They excuse themselves by saying "I've got this weakness and I can't help it." If your weakness is something that defeats you and keeps you defeated in life, you can bet that to continue being weak at that point is not God's will for you. For you, God has something better. What you can't do by yourself God will help you do. As the apostle Paul experienced: "And he said unto me, My grace is sufficient for thee: for my strength is made perfect in weakness" (2 Corinthians 12:9, *KJV*). What you can't do for yourself, let God do in you and through you.

But don't kid yourself, God expects you to do what you can do. You must put forth the effort to do all that you are able; then you can expect God to make up the difference. Stand up to your weakness, look it straight in the eye and say, "I can do all things through Him who strengthens me" (Philippians 4:13 *NASB*).

6. *Accept what you cannot change and with God's help*

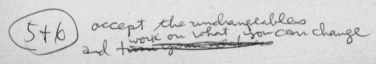
5 + 6 accept the unchangeables and work on what you can change

turn it into something beautiful. The worst thing you can do is to keep rebelling against what has already happened. To do so, is to waste your energies and self away. Healing begins at the moment I say, "God I don't like this, I don't understand it but I accept it as something you have permitted in my life for my growth." God does not cause the hammer to fall on us, that is Satan's attack, but an infinite all-wise God permits suffering to teach us life's greatest lessons. So stop rebelling and let go! Surrender what is so unacceptable to God!

I want to tell you that it does absolutely no good to sit around feeling sorry for yourself. Although it is a temptation, the feeling is real that no one ever had it as rough and tough as you have. Self-pity is the one luxury you cannot afford. Because it does no good, it changes nothing. Worse than nothing, self-pity is harmful. Self-pity does not generate self-respect but further destroys it.

STAND UP AND SLAM THE DOOR ON SELF-PITY

I received a letter from a lady who lives in another state. She wrote, "Years ago I was divorced without scriptural grounds. I remarried about five years ago and became a Christian about one-and-a-half years ago. Questions—what do I do? Am I living in adultery and must I leave my second husband?"

She went on to tell about how that the failure of her first marriage was mainly her fault, but how that her second marriage could be a good one if only she could resolve all this inner confusion that she feels. She shared that she and her husband attended church together and had a great desire to do what God wanted them to do.

After feeling compassion for this woman and praying for her, I wrote to her and said, "Accept what you cannot change and make something beautiful out of it." There are some things she cannot change. She cannot go back and undo a divorce. It would only compound the mistakes to break up what is potentially a happy home that she has now. In spite of what some misguided people may think, it is not God's will for her to live in self-condemnation. There is no sin that any person has ever committed but what God, when we ask, forgives us and sets us free to begin anew.

I said to this dear lady, "Make something beautiful out of what has happened. How do you make something beautiful out of a shattering experience like divorce? Well, first of all, you learn all that you can from it. Then you put the past behind you and in the present do everything that you can, with God's help, to make the present marriage a beautiful and fulfilling relationship."

7. *Put the past behind you.* This is something you have to do not once, not twice, not three times but again and again. By an act of your will, discipline yourself. The other day I did a dumb thing. I was cleaning out some of my files and in one of the files I had kept a couple of letters I had received in the past that had been less than complimentary. I did the dumb thing of getting them out and rereading them. As I did, it brought back old pain. Digging around in past failures only brings up hurt and more hurt. Why do it? It is a dumb thing to do! I am glad to tell you that I finally got smart. I tore up the old letters and threw them away, never to read them again.

I received a letter from some good friends that attended my church in the beginning days of our ministry but moved away to southern Oregon. Here is what the lady shared in her letter: "I must also tell you, Pastor Galloway, that your book, *Dream a New Dream,* helped me shed guilt I felt for several years because my first marriage had failed. Now my husband and I can get on with building a more wonderful relationship."

To wallow around in past failure is not going to help your present situation. Neither is it going to please God. The very best thing you can do for both yourself and your God, is to learn all you can from your failures. Then, shake off the dust of past failure and move ahead to build a new life.

8. *Get up and begin again.* A talented man in his early sixties who had been forced out of the ministry due to some indescretions he had committed said, "Although I knew God had forgiven me, I never believed or hoped that He would ever use my life again until I read your story." Then, with fresh new excitement in his face, he said, "I believe because Jesus lives there is hope for me. I know now that not only has He forgiven me but He wants to use me in a brand new way to bless other's lives." Recently, as I read this verse in Proverbs, I thought about my friend and so many like him who need a fresh new start: "Don't you know that this good man, though you trip him up seven times, will each time rise again?" (Proverbs 24:16, *TLB*).

My friend, no matter what has happened in your life, you can begin to have

A new business,
A new refreshing love,
A return to Christian fellowship,
A new friendship,
A new dream.

YES, YOU CAN
HAVE A FRESH NEW START

4

Stop All
Self-Condemnation

4

Some years ago an uptight mother came to see me, supposedly to talk about her problem child, but ended up blurting out her own acute sexual problem. As she talked, I got the feeling that if I were to allow her to vent her feelings openly she would probably scream bloody murder and scare my fellow staff members in their nearby offices out of their wits.

With great concern she told about how irritable and abusive she had been to her child and how it made her feel like she was a lousy mother. When I questioned her further as to the cause of her emotions getting so out of control, out came her marriage crisis caused by her sexual problem. For months, every time she and her husband would try to have sex together, instead of experiencing pleasure as before, she would experience excruciating pain. A battery of doctors and tests had concluded that her problem did not appear to be physical. One doctor had the audacity to suggest that her problem was purely emotional.

The husband was getting fed up with her sexual problem. She was suffering herself from a lack of fulfillment and anxiety about what was wrong. She recognized that she was taking out her anxieties and frustrations on her child and this was a very bad thing to do. In desperation she cried and pleaded for help.

Responding with compassion, I asked the desperate lady when the pain first started in her marriage act. Reluctantly she recalled that it seemed to have all started right after she had been unfaithful to her husband, one night when he was out of town. It had happened with a man whom she worked with. It really didn't mean anything to her, and she's had little or no contact with the other man since the regrettable one night stand. Here was a guilt ridden lady who was, in her subconscious mind, inflicting punishment and pain upon herself for what she had done wrong. What a privilege it was to introduce her to the forgiveness of the Almighty God, and the weeks that followed to help her to completely accept His forgiveness and to forgive herself. Once she forgave herself, the self-inflicted punishment stopped, and as a result the pain stopped and the pleasure and joy of the marriage was returned.

STOP RUNNING YOURSELF DOWN.
STOP PUNISHING YOURSELF.
HAVEN'T YOU HEARD OF FORGIVENESS?

A prostitute is thrown at the feet of Jesus. Her accusers shout that she is despicable and, according to the law of Moses, she must die. There is no question as to her guilt; she is one of the notorious streetwalkers of their city. Today they seized her in the very act of adultery. Lying on the ground in front of Jesus, she is surrounded by her harsh accusers. They're saying she is unfit to live among them; yet this is not her worst condemnation.

What a way to be introduced to the Holy One, Jesus. Impurity tossed at the feet of purity. The poor miserable creature can't even lift up her head because so heavy is the load—her own guilt and self-condemnation. A long time before she lost all her self-respect. Now all she has left is her sin and shame. Is there anything worse than one's own guilt, condemning conscience?

Keep your eyes on Jesus. What will he say and do? The self-appointed judges are trying to trap Jesus. They think that they have Him caught between the law of Moses and the forgiveness that He has been preaching

In the midst of their accusations and their devilment, Jesus calmly stooped down and wrote with His finger in the sand. "They kept demanding an answer, so he stood up again and said, 'All right, hurl the stones at her until she dies. But only he who never sinned may throw the first!' Then he stooped down again and wrote some more in the dust" (John 8:7, 8, *TLB*).

Aren't you curious? Wouldn't you like to know what He wrote? Whatever it was that He wrote, it couldn't have been more effective in scattering the self-righteous Pharisees than if He had started shooting a shotgun. Because the "Jewish leaders slipped away one by one, beginning with the eldest, until only Jesus was left in front of the crowd with the woman" (John 8:9, *TLB*).

What did He write? Whatever He wrote it was like a miracle ointment because it transformed this defeated, despicable worn out sinner into a fresh, new, respectable woman. What was this powerful life-changing word written in the sand? It was the word that all of us need to hear and understand. A divine word. The word FORGIVENESS!

As Jesus looked at and spoke to this woman, He looked past her sin and shame and saw the beautiful lady she could become with His help, and He said, "Neither do I condemn you; go your way; from now on sin no more" (John 8:11, *NASB*).

"Neither do I condemn you: Go . . . (and) sin no more." Jesus Christ wants to give you freedom from:

Disturbing conscience,
Defeating past,
Damning accusers,
Deflating self-condemnation.

GUILT IS ONE HEAVY TRIP

Suddenly without warning lifetime citizens of the small western town started moving away. It was like a secret plague was on its way and those that knew about it were running for their very life. After a week's time only half of the town's population was left. What a revelation it was when they discovered what had caused so many to flee. A little freckled-face sixth grader by the name of Tommy had mischieviously sent a personal note to every leading citizen in the town. The unsigned note read, "Dear Sir: The game is up, everyone will soon know all about what you did." The fear of being found out can make a person act like an animal that the trap is about to fall on. People do some of the strangest things out of the fear that they will be found out.

Every man and woman alive experiences guilt when he does what he knows to be wrong. Whenever you or I violate our built-in sense of right and wrong, we set in motion the complex emotion of guilt.

Within each of us God has placed an amazing judicial system that we call the conscience. This inner-court only knows two verdicts: guilty or innocent. It knows no gray areas. A man can rationalize his behavior or his bad attitudes, engage in all kinds of fancy self-deception, but he still never fools his own conscience. Once our conscience has pronounced us guilty we must either be forgiven by God and ourselves or our inner-court will keep on demanding punishment. Apart from forgiveness we go on suffering the worst kind of punishment—self-punishment. Can anything be worse than to go on, either consciously or unconsciously, punishing oneself?

Guilt is the most damaging emotion there is. Nothing wipes out self-esteem like guilt. Guilt divides man against himself, against God, against society. The conscience-striken person feels alienated and alone. He cannot live with himself, and he is uncomfortable in the presence of others. It's like he is his own hangman. Guilt ushers fear into one's life. The guilt-ridden man is afraid—afraid of being found out. Guilt caused by unconfessed, unforgiven sins accounts for many of modern man's psychological ills.

What can wash away my sins? Nothing but the blood of Jesus. The difference between being guilt-ridden and forgiveness free is the cross of Jesus. Millions of people have come to know the glorious truth of this chorus—

"At the cross, at the cross, where I first saw the
   light
   And the burden of my heart rolled away,
It was there by faith I received my sight
   And now I am happy all the day"

—Isaac Watts
1674-1748

FOUR THINGS TO DO TO GET OFF THE GUILT TRIP

Man's greatest moment comes when he stops hiding from himself and God and confesses that he is a sinner. It is to Jesus, the compassionate listener and miracle worker, that we are to confess. Anxiously He waits to forgive you, but He cannot forgive and be your Lord until you confess and receive Him. It is the sinner's prayer of confession that opens the ready floodgates of God's forgiveness and floods the soul with forgiveness from sin and freedom from guilt. You need forgiveness and freedom from guilt? Then come to Jesus and confess.

1. *Let Jesus clean your slate.* No doubt you have either

owned, as a child, or have seen a magic slate. You will remember how the slate can be covered with heavy black marks until it looks like it is permanently marked. But then one can lift the sheet and, like magic, the black marks disappear and the slate is clean. This is exactly what Jesus wants to do in our lives. The moment that we confess we are sinners and ask for forgiveness, He wipes the slate clean.

GOD SPECIALIZES IN NEW BEGINNINGS.
MAKE THIS YOUR MOMENT FOR A NEW START.

Not only do each of us need to experience the initial forgiveness and become Christians, but every Christian needs to experience the joy of daily forgiveness. What a shame it is to see good Christian people carrying so much guilt around. How freely God forgives, but He will not forgive the sins that we bury or keep buried. Spiritual breathing is one of the most important principles in the Bible. It teaches us that we are to breathe out, exhale whatever we feel guilty about, and inhale—breathe in God's forgiveness. "If we confess our sins, he is faithful and just to forgive us our sins, and to cleanse us from all unrighteousness" (1 John 1:9, *KJV*).

The more we open up and experience God's freeing forgiveness, the more self-love we will enjoy. Someone has said that, "A man is never whole until he is open to the world." Now this does not mean that a person should stand on top of his house and shout his sins to the world. But it does mean that once we have admitted our wrong and confessed and experienced forgiveness, we no longer have anything to be afraid of having exposed. Therefore, we do not have to live negatively, but we can live positively.

There is a very important principle taught in the New Testament that we practice in our fellowship. Here it is: "Confess your sins (hurts, faults, needs) to one another, and pray for one another, so that you may be healed" (James 5:16, *NASB*). Eloise had obeyed this commandment. It took a lot of courage for her to share her deepest hurts with her Christian friends, but as she poured out the anger that she had felt towards her mother, the group responded in healing prayers and she experienced a healing of forgiveness and freedom from all the guilt. Yes, self-love grows out of openness and honesty. This lady came to have a far better self-image.

2. *Clean up your act.* A young woman wanted to know what to do: whether to go on living with the man that she thought she loved, but wasn't married to, or to leave him and be alone. She wanted to know what I thought. I said, "What do you think?" She began to rationalize, giving all the reasons why she thought it was okay to go on living with this man. Then I asked her, "What does your inner conscience really tell you? How does God feel about this?" She admitted it was sin. She then admitted, too, that she was losing her self-respect. *Sin erodes self-esteem.*

This young woman wanted to get back into fellowship with God. She did not like these worthless feelings that she was having all the time; yet everybody else was doing what she was doing, so why not? What's wrong with it? After all she was a sexual being. Not falling into her trap of self-deception, yet having compassion for her situation, I said lovingly: "If you want your self-respect back; if you want to be close to God; if you want what's best, then you've got to clean up your act. Is having self-respect once again, knowing that you are in the will of God, worth whatever it takes to clean up your act? I believe that it is."

3. *Activate forgiveness in action.* On my desk is a stone that someone gave me a number of years ago. I keep very little on top of my desk to allow room for spreading my

papers all out when I am writing. However, for years now I have kept this stone clearly in sight. Why do I keep it there? To remind me, whenever I am counseling or working with people, of the words of Jesus: "Let him that is without sin cast the first stone" (see John 8:7). I have made up my mind to get off of the judgement seat and live on the mercy seat. As someone has said, "Compassion will cure far more sin than condemnation."

To stop condemning others and start forgiving is to plant good seeds. I have noticed that those who are forgiving in their spirit are the ones who feel the positive flow of forgiveness in their total being. To take the step and, with Christ's help, to forgive others is to set in motion the whirlpool of healing forgiveness for yourself.

4. *Soar to new heights with self-forgiveness*. A number of years ago, a benevolent doctor died. Before his death he went through his books and found many unpaid bills. He realized that the debts had not been paid because the patients were too poor to pay them, so he ran a red line through the record, and then wrote underneath. "Forgiven—unable to pay." After his death, his wife demanded that the patients pay their just obligations. She took the matter to the courts. The judge asked her, "How do you know these people owed this money?" She produced the books. The judge examined them carefully, then handed them back to the doctor's wife and said, "There is no court in the world that will give you a verdict against these people when your husband, with his own pen, has written the words: *'Forgiven*—unable to pay.'"

GOOD NEWS! JESUS WAS NAILED TO A CROSS
SO THAT YOU COULD STOP NAILING YOURSELF
TO A CROSS.

Mary was condemning herself over the last words that she

had spoken to her father before he was killed in an accident. I said to Mary, "Stop it! It's inhuman to keep inflicting yourself with this mental torture over this past mistake. You've asked God to forgive you and He does. It is against God's will to go on punishing yourself." Forgive yourself. It's the only decent thing to do.

For months I had been going over and over the same ground: admitting, confessing, looking at my failures, trying to see where I had gone wrong. All of the failures of a broken marriage were weighing me down. As I was driving down the freeway on a cold day in February, 1971, I saw Jesus hanging on a cross, crying out these words, "My God, my God, why hast thou forsaken me?" There are no more despairing words than these. These words came from a broken man. Then the healing truth hit me. Jesus took all my punishments when he died on that cross. "But he was wounded for our transgressions, he was bruised for our iniquities: the chastisement of our peace was upon him; and with his stripes we are healed" (Isaiah 53:5, *KJV*).

Good News! Jesus took all of my failures, my sins, my shortcomings, the punishment I deserve, when He died on the cross in my place. It was a freeing moment when I accepted the fact that Jesus died to take all my guilt and self-condemnation away. In fact, to go on punishing myself for something I had done wrong or failed to do right, would be to fail to accept all that Jesus Christ did for me when He died in my place on the cross. I have come to love dearly this emancipating verse: "There is therefore now no condemnation to them which are in Christ Jesus" (Romans 8:1, *KJV*).

The grief over the sudden accidental death of an only son, in his teens, would be enough to depress any loving father's heart. But Fred, who sat across the table from me, was suffering from something more severe than the accidental death of his son alone. Since his son's untimely death, seven days ago, he had been teetering back and forth on the brink of suicide. What was it that added mental torture to his broken heart and was driving him nuts? After some gentle probing on my part, we finally got to the root cause when, with much anguish, Fred told how that only three days before his son's death he had become angry and kicked him out of the house. Now the grief, mixed with the guilt was too heavy for my friend to cope with.

I said to Fred, "You know, Jesus is a great healer. Not only does He heal people physically, but He heals them emotionally. Besides that, Jesus is the same yesterday, today and forever. He is the Timeless One. Not only is He present with us here right now, but if you will allow Him to, He will move back into your past and forgive and heal you of what you feel so guilty about now."

With Fred's consent I lead him into an unforgettable experience with the living Christ. I started by asking him to picture in his mind a picture he had seen of Christ. As I was silently praying, Fred fixed his mind on the image and person of Jesus. Then I asked him to see himself standing close to Jesus beside his departed son.

At that emotionally overloaded moment, I helped Fred to openly confess his sin to both Jesus and his son, asking for forgiveness. As I pronounced the words of forgiveness from the Scriptures to Fred, he experienced the warm embrace of Jesus and felt miraculously forgiven by both Jesus and his own son.

Then the grieving father, with my assistance, was able to pray a prayer of relinquishment and place his son in the tender embrace of Jesus. In this healing experience Fred was set free from the unbearable guilt of a past mistake, to begin afresh to live again. With peace in his eyes Fred said to me,

"Isn't the love and forgiveness of Jesus something wonderful?"

Right now, take Jesus into the intimacy of your own sin and guilt. Remember He was crucified for all your guilt hang-ups. See Him as Lord, strong, dependable, and waiting with open arms to receive you and to forgive you. Share with Him what you have been afraid for anyone else to find out. Cry it out—"I was terribly wrong, I sinned, please forgive me." Now, on the authority of God's Word, and in the presence and power of the Living Jesus, accept His complete forgiveness and forgive yourself. Make this freeing verse your verse: "There is therefore now no condemnation to them which are in Christ Jesus" (Romans 8:1, *KJV*).

5

※───◦◦◦◦───※

Experience Inner Healing

5

Just about everybody has some oozing sore spots within them that they need inner healing for. We live in a sea of wounded and hurting people. The truth is that scores of people today need not a little inner healing but a whole lot.

The other day a renowned physician made the statement that the large majority of all people who came to see him were more spiritually ill than they were physically. True, they had physical symptoms—backaches, headaches, skin rashes and other illnesses—but the root cause of their pain and suffering was coming from within. Doctors would be the first to admit that they are not prepared to bring healing to a person's resentments, bitterness, hate, abnormal fears and battered self-images.

The doctors are not the only ones that have been unprepared to deal with man's need for inner spiritual healing. The church, whom God has chosen and appointed to be His agent of spiritual healing on the earth, has been asleep at the switch. All too many churches have been completely blinded to the gift of ministry of inner healing that is theirs to administer in love and with faith. But here and there God is raising up churches that are responding to the challenge of ministering God's healing love to broken people in our fragmented society.

Last year I heard the story of a little nine-year-old girl who lives in California who was viciously sexually assaulted by a perverted man. The girl was not only severely injured, physically, but emotionally shattered. In the excruciating months that followed, a Christian psychiatrist tried all the best methods of psychiatry to bring healing into the little girl's disturbed mind. Many hours and thousands of dollars were spent to no avail. If a man even looked like he was coming close to the little girl, she would go into hysterics.

The psychiatrist invited the family to bring the little girl and attend his church. On Sunday evening at this church great emphasis is placed on the power of God to heal. At the conclusion of each Sunday evening service, all of those who wish to come forward for healing in their lives are invited to come. The mother led the disturbed little girl by the hand down the long aisle. Together they knelt at the altar located at the front of the sanctuary.

One of the men who is an elder in this church is also a renowned surgeon in the Los Angeles area. He is a very compassionate Christian, and has very tender hands. It was in front of him that the emotionally disturbed little girl knelt. This great surgeon, who (by the way) has his entire operating staff pray before every surgery, gently placed his hands on top of the girl's head and in Jesus' name, prayed for her emotional healing. The first part of the miracle was that a man could even place his hands on top of the little girl's head without her becoming emotionally distraught. She remained calm as the doctor prayed. Having finished the prayer, they all stood to their feet. Spontaneously, the little girl threw her arms around the surgeon and kissed him. The audience was immediately filled with tears, knowing that a miracle of God had just taken place.

The following week the Christian psychiatrist, who also was present in the service, examined the girl and recorded that a marvelous emotional healing had taken place in her life. He said that there was no way possible that mere psychiatry could have accomplished, in years, what God could in a moment of faith.

All healing comes from God. One of the things I have been learning is that God uses different instruments to deliver His healing. He uses doctors; He uses ministers; He uses Christian counselors and psychologists; He uses compassionate, concerned Christians in small Bible fellowship groups; and He uses the confession of need and the laying-on of hands by believing Christians praying.

God has a variety of ways of performing His inner healing in a person's life. Sometimes inner healing is instant while more times it is a process—like layers of an onion being peeled back one at a time. Jesus, as the eternal God, knows no time barriers. He knows the future; is present now; and stands ready to move back into any or all of our past experiences of hurt with His healing love touch. There is nothing that has hurt you emotionally or damaged your self-esteem but what Jesus wants to heal and restore to complete wholeness.

Several years ago, in my first book, *Dream a New Dream*, I openly shared my own journey from brokenness to wholeness. It has been very satisfying to hear how God has already used my hurt and healing to give new hope and healing to so many. These testimonials have added joy to my healing.

However, in *Dream a New Dream*, I did not open up my deepest hurt which was the loss of my two children because it still hurt too much. Now I am ready to share with you my deepest hurt—one I didn't think could ever be healed.

"OH GOD! I HURT!"

Blinded by an avalanche of unleashed tears, I somehow managed to back out of my father-in-law's driveway, barely escaping the ditch, onto the snow-covered road. Putting my Dad's new Oldsmobile into the ditch would be a minor accident compared to the crash, bang, break-up that was now tearing my life into shredded wheat.

At the prime age of 31 the dream of being a successful minister like my father was being fulfilled in my life. But now, unlike anyone in my family or circle of conservative church friends, I was caught in the conflict of an unwanted divorce, and I was losing.

A few days before Christmas Sunday, 1970, instead of singing, "Joy To The World," for me there was no joy, and all singing had stopped. My three months of promises and actions to stop being a "work-aholic," and to spend more time at home had fallen on deaf ears. The wipe-out had happened. I was served with the divorce papers, and my unhappy woman took our two children and departed on the airplane—from Portland to Ohio—never to return.

To this day, I do not know how—but somehow I staggered through the Christmas services like a punchy boxer, who had already taken the knockout blow and was still wobbling around on his feet. Sunday night, having stayed and faced the music, I boarded the plane for the East. I went to seek shelter in the warmth and love of my parents' home, and to spend one last Christmas day with my children.

Early Christmas morning I dressed, and ate breakfast with my aging father and mother. This had all been very hard on them. Then I drove the ninety miles to spend Christmas with my son and daughter. At age eight, my son Brian was so much of a man in perception and understanding, and yet—just a little boy. He was my pride and joy, and everything that I wanted in my son. Then there was Lynette:—social, loving and always wrapping her fingers around my heart. How I adored her long dark hair and her big brown, talking eyes.

Christmas day at the home of my estranged wife's parents was something like the many others. Grandpa prayed his traditional prayer before the opening of gifts. As usual, there were many gifts, the playing with toys, and the scrumptious meal. But there was a "clinging" to the children, on my part, and underneath was an unspoken tension that filled the house.

The day passed like a race car. I was powerless to stop the clock or to alter the sentence of grief and divorce that was upon me. The time to say the last "good-byes" came: First it was Lynette that I held in my arms—the last hug; the last desperate kiss; then reluctantly I put my little girl down. I put my arm around my son, and together we walked to the door. There we stopped for one last moment, and unashamedly father and son embraced and kissed. Quickly I turned my back and left, not wanting them to see my grief-stricken face and the unstoppable flow of tears.

Yes, many times I have stood at the graveside of a departed friend or loved one, and felt the loss of an untimely death. But now, the grief and breaking weight of loss of my children was one thousand times worse than I had experienced before. Driving back to my folks' alone, I felt as if my unbearable loss would squeeze the very last breath of life out of me.

In the days to follow, I struggled to learn to live with the continuing pain of my loss. So pricking was this pain, that the only way I could survive and make it through another day was to discipline my thoughts and not allow them to dwell but for a passing moment on my son and daughter.

Several year's later, having rebuilt my life with a strong, happy marriage and a most meaningful, need-meeting ministry of hope for unchurched people, I gave people the impression that I was a whole person again. Thanks be to God! He had picked up the broken pieces and put me back together, and I was whole at every point—except one. Underneath, deep within—where I allowed only my best friend and trusted companion, Margi, my wife, to know me—I was still hurting and broken over the separation from my children.

Before Margi and I had children, shocking as it sounds to me now, I didn't really want to have any more children. And it wasn't because I didn't like children . . . I loved them! But as a result of the hurt and pain caused by the separation from my two children, I did not want to open myself up to be hurt in this way ever again. Many of you understand what I am talking about when I say that being hurt once, I wanted to protect myself from ever being hurt again. The fact was that I was afraid to have children, for fear that the same kind of thing might happen all over again.

Had I centered on my loss and my own hurt, Margi and I never would have had children together. To center on loss, on hurt, on past wrongs, is to just go on hurting . . . hurting . . . hurting!

As I thought about Margi, my wife, whom I love so deeply, I did not want to rob her of the pleasure and joy of bearing children. So much a woman, and so deserving to be fulfilled in the role of motherhood. Still not wanting children for myself, I decided that for her sake, we would have children. I *gave* to Margi. Giving first is the way to turn your sorrow into joy!

April 24, 1974, was one of the greatest days of my life. I was standing there holding Margi's hand as we shared the joy of the birth of our daughter, Ann Margaret. What a joyful experience! How it happened I cannot explain. But at Ann's birth, my deepest nurt was healed by God. My sadness from not having my children was turned to a new joy. What a miracle of inner healing!

Although we love the name Ann (and Ann likes her name,

too), laughingly we often remark that we should have named her Joy! Because bouncing, skipping, laughing, teasing, bubbling—toddler Ann puts joy into her Daddy's daily life. Her mother says Ann and her daddy have something special going.

Now, our baby boy Scottie has come to increase our joy all the more! With him comes so much daily pleasure and great hopes and dreams for the future. Added to all of this is our weekly conversation with my two oldest children, Brian and Lynette, and their anticipated summer visits with us.

Impossible as it once seemed, my deepest hurt is now gone and in its place is the joy of being the father of four beautiful children. Today in my heart is the warm feeling that we are all together as one family in a bond of love even though two of our children live thousands of miles away. I have experienced a miracle of God! He has healed me! Restored all my lost joy—and increased it to overflowing! Thank you, Jesus, for the healing of my deepest hurt.

HOW TO EXPERIENCE GOD'S INNER HEALING FOR YOURSELF

1. *Accept responsibility for your own sins of the spirit.* As far as your own health is concerned—it doesn't matter about the other guy and his sins—what does matter is the condition of your own spirit.

Close friends and acquaintances alike viewed Victor as the "model Christian." His pastor counted him as the lay spiritual leader in their church. Younger men in the church looked up to him as an example of what a man of God should be, as a husband and father. It was a little shocking, to say the least, to those who knew him best to see an ugly spirit erupt like a volcano every time Victor and his wife had a marital spat. It was so out of character for this normally self-controlled and gentle man. The tragedy was that these eruptions would tarnish Victor's witness, disrupt his entire family, hurt his lovely wife, and leave him with a feeling of guilt.

The night after one of his explosions, Victor and his wife attended their Tuesday night home Bible fellowship group. More than anything else, Victor wanted to be the kind of husband that God wanted him to be; so there that night, in an atmosphere of love and acceptance, he dared to open up this ugly spot to God and to concerned fellow Christians. As he talked, something that he had suppressed for years began to surface. Years before, while in dental school, and during the second year of his marriage, his wife had made the mistake of becoming infatuated with her boss. Although this had not been spoken of in years, and Victor thought it was forgiven a long time ago, there had remained a bitterness in his spirit. When confronted with conflict, he cried out for vengeance, saying, "I'll fix her for what she's done to me."

In loving response to Victor's confessed sin, the group prayed and the most wonderful thing happened! Victor's spirit was healed and cleansed of every trace of bitterness. Today he and his wife still have times of conflict and misunderstanding, but gone is Victor's ugly spirit. Because he finally accepted responsibility for it, confessed it as sin to God, he has been forgiven and healed in his spirit.

2. *Visualize Jesus the Lord in prayer by using your God-given imagination.* Right now, fix your eyes on a picture of Jesus that you have seen. Do you see it? Now look into the face of Jesus. Gaze into His eyes. His eyes are so penetrating and commanding, yet they are warm and compassionate. They see it all, they understand everything you feel. Behold His strong arms and see that they are open to you. Jesus is inviting you to come. Hear Him say, "Come unto me all you that labor and are heavy burdened and I will give you help and healing" (see Matthew 11:28).

3. *Picture yuourself once again as a little child, longing to be held and loved.* Allow that inner-most feeling of wanting to be held and loved to come to the surface. Our toddler, Ann, has a common toddler problem of thumb sucking. I guess her thumb tastes pretty good. Her mother has been a little more concerned about it than I am, but we have begun to work together to try to help Ann to get along without sucking her thumb. Ann's attachment to her blanket seems to be connected to her thumb sucking. So, in order to help her cut down on thumb sucking we have been limiting the use of the blanket.

First thing the other morning she came, all teary-eyed, wanting to know, "Where's my blankie?" I said, "Honey, Daddy isn't going to give you your blankie, but I'll give you something better. Here comes Daddy's knee." Ann came and sat on my knee and I hugged her and held her real close, kissed her on the cheek and said, "Ann I love you." You know what? She never said anything more about the blanket. The blanket was just a symptom for a greater need to feel warm, secure and loved.

Walk into the strong arms of Jesus and feel his warm, acceptive, secure embrace. To you, my friend, the Lord says, "I love you—I accept you—I am going to heal you."

4. *Admit to Jesus your helplessness to help yourself.* A woman confided that she wanted to forgive, and she wanted to stop having those hateful feelings toward her ex-husband; but she found herself helpless to change. I said to her, "I'm glad you admit your helplessness." She looked at me as if I was trying to kid her or something. Then I told her how, in my own life, the greatest spritual advances have come when I admitted that I couldn't do it by myself. I need the help of Jesus. How about you?

5. *Open up your deepest wounds to Jesus.* Take Jesus into

every room of your life. Let Him enter those areas where there is fear, where there is disappointment, where there are unspeakable experiences.

The young man said, "I don't understand it. It was the rottenest thing for her to leave me and run off with another man. It's not fair. She should pay for what she's done to me." I replied, "Hey, stop rebelling. Stop holding on to what's eating you up inside. Stop playing judge and jury. Stop destroying yourself with ill feelings. Pour it all out to God."

6. *Ask Jesus to heal you of whatever it is which needs healed.* Spill it out to Jesus. Say to Him what you would not dare to share with any other person. Tell Him what it is that hurts too much to put into words. Join the psalmist in asking God to "Create in me a clean heart, O God; and renew a right spirit within me" (Psalm 51:10, *KJV*).

7. *Forgive whatever it is you need to forgive.* There is no inner healing without forgiveness:

Dave shared with me his struggle to try to practice forgiveness. He had been betrayed by the two people he trusted and believed in the most. The man who was his current business partner, and supposed to be his best friend, was having an affair with his wife. Vengeful thoughts had been going through his mind for days, yet he knew that this was wrong. He even considered putting out a contract to kill, so that he would be rid of the betrayer, have the business free and clear, and have his wife back. These destructive thoughts scared the wits out of him.

Both the lover and the husband were present at a men's retreat for the purpose of developing spiritual leadership. After the evening session on the second day, the lover came to Dave and confessed his sin and asked Dave to forgive him. The man who had hurt him by cutting him to the very core stood there with his hand out, asking for forgiveness and a renewal of friendship. Dave thought, "The nerve of this lowdown scoundrel. He doesn't deserve to ever be forgiven."

Wanting first of all Christ's way in his life, Dave said, "I bowed my head and prayed a quick desperate prayer, telling Jesus about my helplessness to forgive, my inability to love in this situation, about my hate and vengeance, and my ill spirit. Then I concluded by saying, 'Jesus, I cannot forgive him, but you do it through me.'

"Incredible as it would seem to people who do not know Jesus," Dave continued, "my heart flooded with a supernatural wave of love. I saw this man, standing there with his hand out, not as an enemy but as a human being who had failed and was hurting for it, and who needed forgiveness. Christ spoke His words through me, and I said 'I forgive you.' In that moment, we embraced and joyful love flowed. Without Christ, this would never even begin to be possible."

We can love even our enemies with Jesus' supernatural help. The deciding question is not whether you can forgive or not—whether you stop hating or not—whether you can stop the bitterness or not—but the question is: Are you willing to let Jesus help you do what you cannot do by yourself? Let Him forgive through you, let Him love through you.

Forgive that person whom you have hated. Forgive that person you think does not deserve to be forgiven for what they've done. If you do not have the strength in your power to forgive, then ask Jesus to forgive that person through you. Say it out loud, "With Christ's help, I forgive you." Now picture that person in your mind as being forgiven.

8. *Let Christ's healing flow throughout your entire being.* Thank Jesus for what He is doing within you. THANK YOU JESUS.

9. *Commit yourself to new positive action and be whole.* In my inner healing process, a positive action was a commitment to say only good things about those who had hurt me. The second part of my positive action was to commit myself to wishing only good things for those who had hurt me. And, the third part of my commitment for positive action has been, when the opportunity has risen, to help those who had hurt me. Do you know what the results have been? Healthy and good feelings that I enjoy living with. Let me tell you:

GOD DELIGHTS IN TOUCHING
BROKEN PEOPLE AND
MAKING THEM WHOLE!
THANK YOU, JESUS.

6

꒰ঌ◦⚜◦໒꒱

Choose a
Winning Attitude

주변 환경이 민숭해올 때
믿음의 결정에 따라서
환경을 극복하거나
환경의 지배를 받는 되레라고 변함없다

6

More important than what the other guy has,
More important than what has happened to you,
More important than your circumstance,
More important than your education,
More important than money,
More important than fact,
More important than any of these—is your own *attitude.*

How important is your mental attitude? Your mental attitude plays the leading role in every part of your life. It is your mental attitude which either attracts people to you or repels them. It is your own mental attitude that either helps your body to be healthy, or contributes to your ill health. A winning attitude is the difference between those who are victims of circumstances and those, who, with Christ's help, become victors over circumstances.

YOUR ATTITUDE CAN MAKE YOU OR BREAK YOU

Some people today think that the whole world stinks. Once a cranky grandpa lay down to take a nap. To have a little fun, his grandson put some limburger cheese on his mustache under his nose. Grandpa awoke with a snort, charged out of the bedroom and shouted, "This whole house stinks!" He charged out on the porch and shouted as loud as he could,

잠 17:22   마음의 즐거움은 양약이라도 심령의근심
          베르 마르게 하느니라

''The whole world stinks!'' The truth is, it was Grandpa who stunk.

The problem was right under his own nose. Ninety-one times out of one hundred, when we begin to feel like things stink, the problem is not with the world or with others, but ourselves. Our own attitudes have become negative. Change negative attitudes to positive attitudes, and you change your world (see Proverbs 17:22).

Sooner or later everyone has something happen to them that is a heavy blow. It is true—a lot of unfair and unjust things happen in this ol' world. Almost every day I receive a letter or phone call from someone in America who has been broken by divorce. A couple of weeks ago, I received a letter from a man who lives in a northwest state. Before his divorce, he was a very successful man in local government and in business. But now—five years later—he is still defeated and embittered by his divorce. He has allowed what has happened to make shredded wheat out of his life.

From what he wrote in his letter, I would venture to say that most of his continuing difficulties is a result of his own bad attitude.

About the same time, I received a letter from a young woman in Ohio. After briefly telling of her divorce two years ago, she said, ''I praise the Lord for rebuilding my broken life. The lessons that I have learned out of this tragedy have been tremendous.'' After thanking me for my book, *Dream a New Dream*, she ended by saying, ''Well, the Lord has been so good to me since the divorce, and now especially after reading your book of hope, *Dream a New Dream*, I look forward to the future, believing the best is yet to come, with the past behind me.''

I ask you, what is the difference between these two people? They both had the same crushing blow of divorce happen to them. Five years later, the man is still bitter and broken. While the young woman, after two years, is whole and enjoying a positive outlook on life. What is the difference? THE DIFFERENCE IS ATTITUDE!

Who chooses your attitude? You do! The power to choose your attitude is yours. To you, God has given the sole and awesome responsibility of choosing your own attitude. As someone has said, "We are either the master or the victims of our own attitudes. It is a matter of personal choice; blessing or curse." There are many things that happen in your life over which you have no control; you cannot control another person; you cannot control the weather; and often circumstances happen which are beyond our control. But, *you* still choose your own attitudes. And what a difference the choice of your own attitude makes. Scores of people are washed out of the stream of joy in a day simply because they have chosen to have a bad attitude.

A man is literally what he chooses to think, chooses to feel, and what he chooses to believe. For it's these three— THINKING, FEELING AND BELIEVING—that shape and form a man's attitude. And it is our attitude that dictates all of our actions and relationships in our life.

One of the wisest Americans who has ever lived, Ralph Waldo Emerson, said, "A man is what he thinks about all day long." In the Bible it says, "As he thinks within himself, so he is" (Proverbs 23:7, *NASB*). It has been my observation that *those who have a winning attitude are the ones who enjoy living the most:*

They are the ones who win friends and influence people,
They are the ones who overcome whatever comes,
They are the ones who achieve and fulfill dreams,
They are the ones who love life, and it loves them back.

HOW CAN WE HAVE A WINNING ATTITUDE?

① *By choosing to think positive thoughts.*

잠23:7절 에서 그마음의 생각이 어떠하면 그사람도 그러한즉 ......

Every day there comes into each of our minds many positive thoughts and negative thoughts. The choice as to which ones stay in your own mind is yours. If you are to get the best results in life, you must be selective as to what you put into your mind and to what you allow to dwell there. The thoughts that you choose this day will work to either give you a negative life or a positive one. To not exercise your choice is to allow negative thoughts to seize control of your mind. Negative thoughts are self-defeating. To say, "I can't," stops a man before he even gets started. To think the worst of another person is to separate you from the person that could be your very best friend. Negative thoughts can make you sick, and often do make people ill.

I love one of Dr. Norman Vincent Peale's stories from a sermon entitled *Creative Help For Daily Living*, in which he told about a talented and beautiful woman who thought herself into becoming an invalid. Oh, she had both beauty and brains but she refused to stop thinking about the fact that she had come out of a poverty-striken family. Her husband came from one of the so-called "best" families and had gone to one of the finest schools in the East. Although she was a very brilliant young lady she had never gone past high school and when she married this man who had so many advantages, she had a great sense of inferiority. As time passed on she began dwelling on how inferior she thought she was until she actually made herself sick. Her subconscious mind told her, "You can't keep up with your husband's success. But maybe, if you act sick, it will make him have sympathy for you and he will have to care for you and love you all the more."

So, as Dr. Peale tells the story, she proceeded to get sick—thinking that was how she would hold on to her husband. She was waited on hand and foot. In a way this all pleased her because now she was the center of attention.

The wise doctor who was handling the case understood what was going on and so he told the husband, "This is preposterous. I find nothing wrong with her. The trouble is in her own inner-thought life. She thinks she is sick, so she is." The doctor suggested something which sounds amusing, but it worked.

The doctor hired a nurse who had been a beauty queen. She was a real glamour girl, just as lovely and sweet as could be, (and a little younger than the wife, too). So this lovely nurse took care of the woman, and in caring for the patient she got to know the husband real well.

One day the doctor ordered the husband to say to his wife, "Sweetheart, you have been telling me you are going to die pretty soon and this breaks my heart. But," he continued, "I want you to know that I think I found someone to take your place. You have often said how you want me to be happy and well cared for after you are gone. Your concern for me touches my heart. I want you to know that I find our nurse very attractive. With your blessing, when you're gone, I think I would like to marry her." That did it! That woman got right up out of bed, made the nurse pack her bags and proceed right out of the house. Miraculously the wife became a well woman. She no longer lets thoughts of inferiority dominate her. Finally one day she told her husband why it all happened: "I always felt inferior to you," she confessed.

"I can't imagine why," her husband said. "I love you for what you are, a sweet and wonderful woman. I can't imagine living without you." The woman realized at last just how much she was loved. Because she eliminated destructive thinking, her life became new and wonderful. Jesus wants to replace the losing attitude with the winning attitude.

Here is what God Himself, tells us to do to eliminate the destructive negative, "Don't worry about anything; instead,

I can't but O can!!

빌 4:6-9

pray about everything; tell God your needs and don't forget to thank him for his answers'' (Philippians 4:6, *TLB*). In other words, pour out all the negative to God, get rid of it.

Then the Scripture says, "If you do this you will experience God's peace, which is far more wonderful than the human mind can understand" (Philippians 4:7, *TLB*).

Select the positive and dwell on it. Here's what the next part of that says: "Fix your thoughts on what is true and good and right. Think about things that are pure and lovely, and dwell on the fine, good things in others. Think about all you can praise God for and be glad about. Keep putting into practice all you learned . . ." (Philippians 4:8, 9, *TLB*). What is it we are to do? We are to fix our thoughts on the positive. That is an action we are to take. We are to think about things that are pure and lovely. That's something we choose to do daily, moment by moment. Then it tells us we are to dwell on the fine, good things in others. That word "dwell," is a big one. Question: What are you dwelling on? Whatever you dwell on is what is going to capture you. To cultivate a positive attitude we must dwell on the good.

Then, the Scriptures exhorts us to keep putting these things into practice. It is not something you do once and stop, but it is something that we must do again and again and again—daily, hourly, minute by minute. This is Christ's superior way for us to think "right." And choosing to think right is the first step in having a winning attitude.

HOW CAN WE HAVE A WINNING ATTITUDE?

By choosing right feelings.

For some unknown reason to me, lately I have been getting sworn at by other drivers in traffic. The first time this happened to me about ten days ago—and I still don't know why—a lady cursed me. I kind of just laughed at it.

A couple days later, I pulled out in front of a man, thinking
I had lots of time. He swung his car around to the left of me
and passed; and as he did, he looked at me, shook his fist,
and called me some unmentionable names. To tell the truth, I
didn't like it; but, I kept looking straight ahead, biting my
tongue and not reacting.

Then last Monday night, driving with my family, I did
something which evidently didn't please a man driving
behind me in a pickup truck. At the next traffic light he
pulled up beside me and there, right in front of my family,
called me the dirtiest name you can call anyone. I want to tell
you that this unjust treatment made me angry! Being a
Christian and a pastor, I certainly couldn't use abusive
language like he was addressing me, so I did the next best
thing: I clenched my fist and, half joking and half mad, I
shook it at him. My wife, Margi, looked at me and said,
tongue in cheek, "That was nice Christian behavior." You
better believe I felt awfully ashamed at what I had done.

We arrived at our friend's house, where we were to have
dinner and spend the evening; and while we were waiting for
dinner, Margi picked up a devotional book that was on the
table. On the first page she turned to, at the top of the page,
was this verse (which she politely put her finger under and
showed me): "So then everyone of us shall give account of
himself to God" (Romans 14:12, *KJV*). Then the spiritual
truth that I had temporarily forgotten hit me like a ton of
bricks! I am not responsible for the other person's wrong
attitude or actions, but I am responsible to God for my own.
No matter what the other guy did wrong, there was no excuse
for my misbehavior out of a wrong spirit.

What do you do when someone has done you wrong? What
do you do about the other guy? The Scriptures tell us what to
do: "Dear friends, never avenge yourselves. Leave that to
God, for he has said that he will repay those who deserve it.

(Don't take the law into your own hands)'' (Romans 12:19, *TLB*). You leave the other guy to God.

I am responsible for my own spirit. A winning attitude comes out of a right spirit. Proverbs 16:32 tells us: "He who is slow to anger is better than the mighty, and he who rules his spirit, than he who captures a city" (*NASB*).

A young Christian woman confessed that she had had terrible bitterness inside towards some other Christian people. She knew that the bitterness was wrong and that it was not good for her; but she told the Lord that she wanted to hang on to it just a little longer, so she could enjoy it. Finally, however, she came to her good senses and admitted to herself that there was no way that any real enjoyment comes out of holding on to bitterness. Bitterness is destructive, in any form. Worst of all, it mars and damages the person who holds on to it.

What do you do when you have an ill spirit? When there is bitterness or resentment? You must do what this young lady did. You confess the sin of harboring these feelings to Jesus Christ. You let go of it, and you let Him have it. You put the unforgivable situation in His hands, and you turn the person that you have been hating over to God. You confess your wrong attitude and you ask for Jesus' forgiveness. How beautiful, how cleansing, how freeing, how lifting is the forgiveness Jesus gives to everyone who confesses and asks to be made whole in spirit. "Let this mind be in you, which was also in Christ Jesus" (Philippians 2:5, *KJV*).

Some friends of ours, Phil and Judy DuFresne, got a new pickup truck. And like any of us, when we get a new vehicle, they were really proud of it, and had every right to be.

Phil, who's a trucker, drove his new pickup to work; and while he was out trucking, one of the young drivers backed into his brand new pickup! How would you like to have your new truck backed into? When Phil came back in, his boss and the other drivers all "baited" him into having a bad attitude. They said, "If it were me, I'd beat up on that young punk!" . . . or . . . "What a jerk! Backing into your new truck!" . . . or . . . "That #&!*&†! kid!"

Well, Phil refused to take the bait. He's learning that a bad attitude is one thing he can't afford, so he turned something negative into something positive: He said, "You know, I think it really took a lot of courage for that young man to confess that he was the one that did it. He could have been like so many and just gone on and not ever told anyone." Phil's fellow truck drivers, who knew him years before Jesus came into his life, just stood there with their mouths hanging open.

Every time we show a good attitude in a crisis, we give a beautiful witness to what Jesus is doing in and through our lives. The worse the abuse, the greater the opportunity to show the power of Christ at work within your attitude.

Show me a man or woman who—regardless of what happens to them—refuses to allow themselves to have a bad attitude, and I will show you a person who is going to come out on top.

HOW CAN WE HAVE A WINNING ATTITUDE?

By believing "right."

The most important thing about me is what I believe. I've heard it said that it doesn't matter what you believe. However, nothing could be further from the truth because what you believe determines what you are. Your belief determines where your life is going. On one occasion Jesus said, "All things are possible to him who believes" (Mark 9:23, *NASB*). Someone has said: "Your belief determines the possibilities of your life." It is absolutely amazing what believing can do in your life.

The third step to a winning attitude is to believe "right" about God, about yourself, about others and about the final outcome of a difficult situation. The place to begin beginning believing "right" is to believe that God is on your side. Jesus came that we might have life and have it more abundantly. "Whatever is good and perfect comes to us from God . . ." (James 1:17, *TLB*). It is God's wish that, "Above all things that thou mayest prosper and be in health, even as thy soul prospereth" (3 John 2, *KJV*). God is on your side. He wants to make you more than conquerors. Ask yourself this question from Scripture: "If God is on our side, who can ever be against us?" (Romans 8:31, *TLB*). As someone has said: We must not only believe in God; but *believe* God.

Look at your enemies, look at your problems, look at your situation and be defeated. Look to God, your Source as your Help, the One that has all power and get a winning attitude.

After having been slaves in Egypt, the children of Israel had a bad attitude. They were beaten, they were defeated. They believed themselves to be no better than slaves. They lived negatively in their fears. Moses looked at them and he saw them as children of God who could become free men instead of slaves, who had tremendous potentials and possibilities. Thus it was that Moses became the chosen leader of God to lead the people out of Egyptian bondage.

Faced with the immovable Red Sea and the Egyptian soldiers closing in on them from behind, the people looked at their insurmountable problem, then grumbled at Moses and said, "Why didn't you leave us alone?" But Moses looked to God, the All Powerful One who was his Source, and he said, "The Lord will fight for you, and you won't need to lift a finger!" (Exodus 14:14, *TLB*).

"Then the Lord said to Moses, 'Quit praying and get the

people moving! Forward, march!'" (Exodus 14:15, *TLB*).
The Lord told Moses to use what he had, to hold his rod out
over the water. Moses did this and God did the rest. He
opened the Red Sea, rolled the water back, and the people
walked on through on dry ground. "With men it is
impossible, but not with God: for with God all things are
possible" (Mark 10:27, *KJV*). 창 18 :14 *Is there anything too difficult for ⊙ ?*

Recently someone asked me how I made it through the
double tragedy of family break-up and ministerial failure
seven years ago—now, to rebuild a rich, fulfilling family life
and an effective ministry of new hope to so many people. The
reason, I believe, that God could help me rebuild and come
out on top was that I determinedly refused to stop believing
in God. Believing that God is bigger than all my problems.
Believing that God loves me and I am a child of God.
Believing that God will bring something good out of the
worst. Believing that God would use my pain to bring future
gain. Believing that God had many lessons to teach me
through it all, and that He was not finished with me yet. Yes,
believing that in spite of what anyone said, that God still
wanted to use my life to minister. I can tell you from my
firsthand experience, ". . . all things are possible to him who
believes" (Mark 9:23, *NASB*). Believing will raise the
altitude of your attitude. Nothing is impossible when you put
your trust in God. You, too, can have a winning attitude.

삶에 어떤 상황에 닥들지
나분 명가, 나뿐 감정을 억제하고
은해를 라세놓은 지라토라
은혜라노 자의
비결.

7

Turn Your Failures
Into Stepping Stones

7

I have to admit that I'm not real sure that I want to write this chapter. You understand, it's not that I don't enjoy writing because I do. But if I'm honest about my feelings, I am just a little bit scared to reveal myself so openly by sharing with you some of my failures. For a person like myself who has been very success oriented, it's not easy to privately face my own failures, let alone publicly put them on display.

Failure scares the wits out of me! Failure is like a thief that comes at night and sneaks into the privacy of our homes and robs and steals away that which we want most. It seems that sooner or later everyone is robbed by the villain of failure. It is a nauseating feeling when failure has come and left, leaving you alone with your loss.

Recently, I counseled with a man who is being defeated by his failures. To have failed is bad enough, but to be convinced that you are a failure, to have surrendered to a failure complex, is to be beaten to a pulp.

GOD CREATED YOU TO BE A PRINCE, NOT A BEATEN PAUPER.

This man with the failure complex not only expressed his own experience but the experience of many when he said, "My life has been like dominos falling, one on top of the other. My life has been failure, failure, failure, in an unending succession.''

Struggling to find a way out from under this failure complex, the man begged me to tell him how to get rid of the feeling that he was the world's biggest failure.

Identifying with this hurting individual, and feeling strong compassion for him I said, ''I, too, know what it is to drink the bitter cup of failure. The taste of failure is enough to fill anyone with bitterness.

''Like you, I know what it is to have failed in a marriage. To feel like a failure as a lover and husband. To hate yourself because by being partner to a marriage failure, you have failed your own innocent children. When divorce happened to me I interpreted that to mean that I was one big failure.

''Like you, my friend, I know what it is to have failed in an occupation. Let me tell you, it is a devaluing experience to be a pastor without people to pastor. After years in the ministry, I found myself with no job. Worse yet, there didn't seem to be any congregation that wanted me. Yes, my friend, I know what a horrible feeling failure is. Like you, I hate being a failure.''

Because of this man, and many like him, I have decided to go ahead and run the risk of openly sharing with you many of my failures. I do this because I believe that you can identify with a life that has had some failures. It is my prayerful intention that from my doing this, many of you, too, will face up to your failures and with God's help experience personal growth.

I would never dare to open myself up in this matter if I had not been helped by Christ, Himself, to learn so many lessons from my failures that are presently filling my daily life with new joy. Joy-filled living is the product that has come from the lessons born out of my failures.

Believe it or not, failure may be your—

Blessing in disguise,
Doorway to new opportunity,
Teacher of priceless lessons,
Enricher of personality,
Pathway to a richer fellowship with God,
Stepping stone to true success.

As bad as it seemed at the time, not everything about my divorce was bad for me. One positive thing that my shocking divorce did for me was to force me to take a long hard look at myself. Under the microscope of self-examination, I began to see areas of failure to which I had been totally oblivious. Thus, as a direct result of my divorce failure, I opened up to God for change and personality growth in my life in a way that I had never done before.

What is failure? One thing for sure, it is something just everybody experiences at one time or another. Yet it is the one thing none of us want in our life. I personally hate to fail, don't you?

HERE ARE NINE THINGS YOU NEED
TO KNOW ABOUT FAILURE

1. *To fail is not the same as being a failure*. How quick we are on the trigger to jump to the wrong conclusion and brand one who has had failings as a forever failure. Just because an individual has failed here, there, and yonder, does not automatically mean that he or she is a failure.

One may have many failings and yet still be far from being a failure. A failing is a failing, nothing more, nothing less. When a person has failed it does mean he has not yet succeeded in what he set out to accomplish. It does mean that something has gone wrong. It does mean that to overcome and succeed he is going to have to dig in and try harder the next opportunity. Remember this, life is so much more than a few failings here and there.

Edmund Vance Cooke has, in these penetrating words, given to us a positive way of defining the word failure:

"What is failure? It is only a spur
To the one who receives it right.
It makes the spirit within him stir
To go in once more and fight.
If you never have failed, it's an easy guess
You never have won any high success."

2. *To fail is not the disgrace everyone thinks it is.* I wonder where we ever got it in our head that to fail was disgraceful. Somewhere along the line this false concept has set up in our minds like hardened concrete. It is this false concept—to fail is a disgrace—that we need to break up and unlearn.

You see, if failing by itself were disgraceful, then everyone of us are prime examples of disgrace. Isn't it true that all of us have had more failures than we like to admit? Isaiah 53:6 says, "All we like sheep have gone astray; we have turned everyone to his own way; and the Lord has laid on him the iniquity of us all" (*KJV*).

To err is to do nothing more than to join the human race. It goes along with our humanness and is a part of the total human situation. Admittedly, trial and error is one of the methods for learning. However, it is much easier and neater if we can learn without having to personally experience every failing known to man. Although when we do fail, we who know God can cooperate with Him in allowing Him to use even our failings to build our character. The next time that you or another person has failed, remember this principle, "To fail is human, to forgive is divine."

3. *Failure is only a temporary setback.* Failure is never the final chapter of the book of your life unless you give up and quit. View failings in your life as temporary setbacks to future advances.

너 또 그랬니?

Because you have failed in a past marriage does not
mean you cannot succeed in a future one.
Because you have lost a battle or two does not mean
you cannot win the war.
Because you have experienced a business failure
does not mean you cannot succeed in future business.
Because you've been turned down by one school
does not mean you will not be accepted in
another school.
Because you have been branded as a failure by one
church does not mean you will not be
accepted in warm restoring love by another
church.
Because you have failed the driver's test does not
mean you cannot take it again and again
until you pass it.

Never allow yesterday's failures
To wipe out the possibilities of tomorrow's successes.

A man is never a failure in God's sight until he gives up
and quits trying. Someone has said: "A winner never quits,
and a quitter never wins."

4. *Nothing worthwhile is ever achieved without running
the risk of failure.* The man who risks everything to try to
achieve something truly worthwhile and fails is anything but
a disgraceful failure. He has had the courage and the guts to
go down trying.
To me, a failure is a person who either never tries or, after
a few failings, allows the fear of failure to seize control and
stop him dead. Whatever you do, don't take yourself out of
the action by succumbing to the fear of failure.
The fear of failure is something that with Christ's help we
must all stand up to. Stand up to your fears of failure with

faith, and the death of those fears are certain. I have come to
love and live by the familiar words of my friend and
renowned minister, Dr. Robert Schuller, when he says, "I
would rather attempt something great and fail, than attempt
nothing and succeed." It was because of these words that,
after my experiencing a marriage failure, I took the risk of
marrying again. It was because of these words that I ran the
risk of failure by starting New Hope Community Church
without any people. I want to tell you, I am so glad that I
didn't surrender to my past failings and my very real fears of
failing.

5. *Failure is a natural preparation for success.* Strange as
it may seem to some of you, success is much more difficult to
live with successfully than is failure. It takes a lot of character
to be successful—as people of this world view success—and
still be a warm, relating person.

My friend and associate in the minstry of New Hope, Rich
Kraljev, previously worked for ten years for an Airlines. The
other day he was telling me how it was his job to meet a lot of
famous people, to see that they were given the red carpet
treatment. Many of them were often arrogant, demanding
and downright rude to the people serving them. You see, not
everyone is ready to live with success.

The physical laws that God has built into our universe tell
us that failure is a natural preparation for success. As a
toddler everyone of us failed many times in our first attempts
to walk. Nevertheless, it was through these feeble attempts
that our legs gained strength. It was by failing and trying
again and again that we became successful in walking.

I have never seen a man or woman yet who was able to live
well with success who had not first traveled through the fires
and storms of failure. It is failure that keeps a man
remembering, when he is successful, how other people hurt

and feel. No individual is truly successful who does not share his success with others and help all those who have failed to also experience the joy of success.

6. *Every failing brings with it the possibilities of something greater.* Analyze failure under whatever circumstances you choose, and you will discover some seeds for turning failure into success. Although a juicy, delicious apple may have turned rotten and lost its delicious taste, there still remains within that apple, the seeds to produce apple trees.

Alexander Graham Bell was married to a woman who was hard of hearing. His love for her and his desire for her to hear drove him into many endless hours of research. He faithfully worked many years to create a mechanical hearing aid for his beloved. But all of his perspiration and hard work failed to come up with a hearing aid. It appeared that Bell had completely failed. And yet out of this apparent failure was born the greater success of the long distance telephone.

If you are going to accomplish worthwhile goals in your life, you can expect some failings. But when this happens, train your mind to look immediately for the seeds of something greater for you to do. To turn all your failings into successes: Strive to do something greater than you have ever done before.

7. *Reassuredly, the Bible is full of thrilling stories of how God used people who had failed.* It seems like just about any personality that you want to study in the Bible either personally was a failure or came out of a failure situation to be used by God. One cannot read the Bible with an open mind without seeing that God does not turn His back on people who have failed, but rather He forgives them, strengthens them and uses them to do wonderful things in His Kingdom work. Classsic examples are: Moses, Samson, Jonah, David, Mark, Peter, and the other disciples, to sight a

few. If God used men of old after they failed, don't you believe He can still use us today in spite of our failures?

8. *What you do with failures in your life is up to you*. Failure is either a blessing or a curse, depending upon the individual's reaction or response to it. Failure can be a stick that you can use to beat yourself to death or, on the other hand, failure can be a stick to prod you on to greater success. Failure can be something that makes you draw nearer to God, to be perfected in your weakness. God delights in making successes out of failures, turning defeats into victories.

Abraham Lincoln was a failure many times before he became a famous man in history. History tells us that he failed in storekeeping, surveying, soldiering, and in the practice of law. Lincoln failed so miserably in business that it took him seventeen years to pay off the debts of a worthless partner. Entering into politics, he failed first in his bid for the Illinois Legislature; next, he was defeated in his campaign for Congress. In 1856 he was defeated in his run to be Vice-President.

Every one of these failings and more were used to shape, form and build strong character into Abraham Lincoln. It was the failings in his life from which he learned so much. They prepared him to be the President during the worst crisis in American history. Failure brought the best out of the greatest President of the United States, Abraham Lincoln.

9. *Failings are opportunities to learn how to do things better the next time—to learn where the pitfalls are and how to avoid them.* I have learned so much more from my failings than I have from my successes, that I want to share my lessons with you. The best possible thing to do with failure, I think, is to learn all you can from it.

LIFE-CHANGING LESSONS I'VE LEARNED FROM MY FAILURES

FAILURE ONE: I put my goals and work as a minister in the church ahead of my family.

LESSON: That I must put my family ahead of my church work. One day I was reading in The Living Bible when I came across these words that have literally turned my life upside-down with change: "Let love be your greatest aim" (1 Corinthians 14:1).

My confession is that for years I had, with the best intentions, lived with mixed up priorities. I thought I was doing right by putting the church first in everything I did, while all the time I was neglecting my wife and children. During this period of time in my life, in spite of the fact that I had worked all day long and many previous evenings, when I did take an evening at home with the family I would feel guilty for not being at work. Then, when I had been out working night after night, I would begin to feel guilty because I wasn't at home. As a result of putting the church ahead of the family I was on a guilt-trip all the time. You see, when your priorities are mixed up, no matter how sincere you might be, the result (in terms of daily life) is confusion and chaos.

I've come to see that the most important goal in life is to make love my number one aim. The way this works out is that my family must come ahead of my church work. People and relationships are to be more important than the programs. In fact, I've come to believe that a successful ministry, the kind that is lifting, healing, building and enduring, comes out of love relationships. The kind of love that begins at home with the members of our family and then spreads to the other people that we are closest to in our relationships. Only a church where people are taught to make love their number one aim, by both the sermon and pastoral example, can begin to meet the deep needs that we all have today.

In the summer of 1976, our youngest child, Scott, was born—right in the middle of a week of heavy evening commitments for me. I realized that the time to share this precious experience of the birth of our newborn baby was right then. During the three days my wife was in the hospital, she needed me and I needed to be with her to fully enjoy this special time together. So you know what I did? I canceled out the first night; I had my associate take the second night; and one of our leading board members filled in for me the third night. The amazing thing was that none of the work of the church suffered while Margi and I enjoyed a very close time of fellowship together on each of these three evenings spent in the hospital.

Do you know that when a person is making love his number one aim there is no way on this earth that he can ever end up being a failure? It's true, you may fail in a business deal; you may lose your job; you may even end up with some broken relationships, simply because it takes two people to have a relationship. But, if you keep on making love your number one aim, you will never be a failure, because the Bible says, "Love never fails" (see 1 Corinthians 13:13).

On the other hand, you may succeed in climbing to the top of your profession; you may achieve earthly fame and fortune but if you end up without love, what do you have?

FAILURE TWO: I was a workaholic.

LESSON: To get the most out of living life, I must be balanced between laughter and seriousness, work and play. I used to be so enslaved to work that I didn't even see the roses, let alone take time to smell them. Then one day I was looking at some roses and seeing them in their beauty for, I think, the first time. The thought came to me: "Who made these roses?" The answer was simple, God did. Then the question came: "Why did he make them?" The answer, He made them for my pleasure and enjoyment. *Take time to smell the roses in your life.*

I was such a workaholic that even when I would attend a party given by the young couples in our church, I would never let down and relax and enjoy myself. Always I had to be working, plotting, planning, getting someone off to the side, selling them on a new idea or program that I wanted to get across.

All work and no play not only made Dale a dull boy, but it made him intense and a transmitter of tension. God has taught me that the way to reduce tension and to live more relaxed is to turn off the work completely and fully enjoy times of play. It is so much fun to relax, to laugh and to enjoy family members and friends. As the ancient writer in Old Testament wisdom put it: "There is a right time for everything . . . a time to plant . . . a time to laugh . . ." (see Ecclesiastes 3:1-13, *TLB*). What a transforming realization it was to realize that God loved me when I was laughing and playing just as fully as He did when I was doing His work. The amazing thing is that I'm finding that I get far more accomplished in my work when I keep relaxed than when I forget to take time to play, allowing myself to become too intense. When I get all tight inside, I start sending out tension vibrations to others. And that is the exact opposite of what I desire to do for the people I minister to who live in an uptight world.

FAILURE THREE: In the past I was a very poor listener. Why? Because my mind was often preoccupied with some idea or thing that I was going to say or do.

LESSON: The all-importance of needing to work on becoming a good listener. This lesson didn't come easy. First of all, I had to learn to stop thinking about what I was going to say next while someone else was talking. Then, I had to learn to bring my concentration to bear on what that person was saying. One of the things I've discovered is that as I earnestly listen to another individual, with interest and interact, they respond more favorably to me. Thus I am building more quality relationships with people. The more I listen to people, the more I love them; the more I listen.

Just the other day one of the young women in our church who knew me back seven or eight years ago, paid me a very meaningful compliment. She said, "Dale, I really appreciate what a good listener you have become." My friend, with God's help, you too can turn a weakness into a strength.

FAILURE FOUR: As a husband I failed at two very important points. The first point was that I did not accept and validate my wife's feelings as being important; and the second failure was that I did not put any importance at all on taking care of our house and property.

LESSON: I do not have to always be so acutely logical, or preach a 30-second sermon, but can simply accept my wife's feelings. I have learned that when Margi hurts or is upset that what she needs from me is a warm acceptance of her emotions. What I do when she is hurting is to hold her, to listen and to validate her feelings as being okay and being very important to me. Sometimes I still have to bite my tongue to resist the old temptation to correct or give advice. But because I have learned to validate my wife's feelings, Margi would tell you that she knows, without a doubt, that I am in her corner when she needs me and she feels like I understand her. Isn't that interesting in light of the old adage, "Who ever understands a woman?"

LESSON: I am learning to pay attention to the upkeep and improvement of our house and property. In the past, I could walk in and out of our broken screen door for days and never see it. After having it called to my attention again and again,

I still wouldn't see any need to be in a big rush to make the repairs. God has taught me that a part of caring for my wife and children is to keep the home in good repair and to keep on making improvements. The most amazing thing has happened in my life: Things that I thought I could never do, I have found out that I can do. The payoff is that when I fix things, I feel good. I am actually beginning to enjoy fixing up and beautifying our home. If it were not happening to me, I never would have believed it.

FAILURE FIVE: I have learned that marriage is something that I have to *work at* to keep it up-to-date and working. One of the big dangers that ministers and their wives face is that they will give so much of themselves emotionally to other people that they have nothing left to give to meet their mate's emotional needs. If ministers and their wives were honest with you, they would tell you that they have more difficulties getting along with each other on Monday than any other day of the week. Why is this? It is because they are both emotionally spent after a day of emotionally giving to others on Sunday. The day after finds two emotionally drained people, each looking to the other for a lift, yet neither has anything left to give.

I am learning to keep on working at my marriage relationship and to not take my good wife for granted; to reserve time and energy to try and meet the needs of the woman I love, Margi.

FAILURE SIX: In the past I was too quick to judge other people for their sins and failures.

LESSON: I have learned through my own failure and to leave the judging to God; to keep on loving and believing in people in spite of their failures. With God's help, people do change for the better.

FAILURE SEVEN: In the past I wasn't as sensitive and compassionate to people who were hurting as I should have been.

LESSON: God has taught me to feel with people who hurt; to be so sensitive as to look in their eyes and see the emotions they are feeling; and, most of all, to show them the compassion and love of Jesus.

FAILURE EIGHT: For years I went on oblivious to my own weak spots and failures, all the time kidding myself into thinking that I was being a good husband, father and worker for God.

LESSON: I do have failures in my life, areas I need to improve in, things I need to change. I have learned that the day I quit learning, I stop growing. With God's help, I have changed; I am changing; and I will continue to change for the better. Learning from failures is making my motto, ''The best is yet to come,'' a reality in my life.

TURN YOUR FAILURES INTO SUCCESSES.

You, too, can turn your failures into successes! How? By learning all you can from your failures and using them as stepping stones.

배움의 중단은
성장의 중단을 뜻 한다

8

❧～✤～❧

Things You Can Do to Feel Good About Yourself

8

자아를 어떻게 보는가?
Nobody to
Somebody

What shall it profit a person if he gain fame, fortune and position, yet feel crumby about himself as a person? Is there anything more important to you than how you feel about yourself as a person? Everywhere you go, whatever you do, the way you feel inside about yourself goes with you. To feel good about yourself as a person is a terrific, exhilerating feeling! But to feel worthless is not only a terrible feeling, but it is self-defeating.

Every one of us can improve the way we feel about ourselves. Just because you have not felt good about yourself as a person does not mean you cannot experience a new birth of self-worth. It does mean that you are going to have to make a conscious effort and work at it. As we have been learning together, throughout this book, feeling like a somebody again comes as a result of eliminating negative feelings about oneself and choosing and cultivating positive feelings of self-worth. Let me caution you: Do not expect an instant transformation! But recognize that it takes a great deal of time, with Christ's help and your concentrated effort, to realize continuing good feelings about yourself.

The greatest truth in all the world is also the simplest. It is this foundational truth upon which everything I have said in this book is built. This is it: GOD LOVES YOU—GOD LOVES

자아기 과점
부정적 인
자세를
없에고
긍정적인
부음을
카시
함양
해야한다

빌1:6 너희속에 착한(선한)일을 시작하신 이가
그리스도 예수의 날까지 이루실 줄을 우리가
확신하노라.

ME—GOD LOVES US. God's will for your life will not be
fulfilled until you feel like a somebody. God created you to be
a somebody. Jesus Christ came to restore you to being a
fulfilled child of God. As you put forth the effort and
cooperate with God to become the wonderful person He has
created you to be, remember this promise: ''God who began
the good work within you will keep right on helping you grow
. . .'' (Philippians 1:6, *TLB*).

EIGHT THINGS YOU CAN DO
TO FEEL GOOD ABOUT YOURSELF

1. *Be yourself.* I heard one of America's best known news
commentators, Paul Harvey, tell this experience. Years ago,
as a young newscaster just starting out, he found himself
trying to imitate the different well-known newscasters that
he idolized. Intently, he would listen to one of his heroes;
then, he'd go on his own broadcast, trying to imitate the
famous newscaster. Fortunately for Paul Harvey, a frank
director pointed out the truth to him: ''Paul, when you're
trying to be like someone else you're always going to come
out second best.'' Right then and there Paul Harvey made up
his mind to stop imitating other greats and be himself.
Across the years he has developed his own style and
technique to perfection. As a result, today Paul Harvey is
anything but second best. You, my friend, were not created
to be second best to anyone else—you were made to be the
best *you* possible.

Be yourself and you will have no need to compare yourself
with anyone else. Fulfilled persons are those who accept
themselves and work hard to develop their abilities to the
fullest. You have unlimited potential! You have every right to
be proud of who you are and what, with God's help, you are
becoming.

In a home Bible fellowship group that meets in our home,

남은 인생을 하나님 안에서 우리도 항상 그들 앞에서 옳으리라.

갈 6:4 "각각 자기의 일을 살피라 그리하면
자랑 할 것이 자기에게만 있고 남에게는 있지
아니하리니 …"

충족된 없는 자기 의식이나 가치가 무한함을 깨닫고
무조건 가치를 발견하라 깨닫아 남보다 예만 가능하다

비교하지 맙시다.

we read together from Galatians this special verse, "Let
everyone be sure that he is doing his very best, for then he
will have the personal satisfaction of work well done, and
won't need to compare himself with someone else"
(Galatians 6:4, *TLB*). As we shared this verse together,
someone in our group made this meaningful insight: As a
person is busy developing his own potential, growing into the
person God created him to be, there comes such a personal
satisfaction that there is no need to compare himself to
someone else.

DO YOURSELF A FAVOR:
BE YOURSELF

숫가 들놀이 높은 일한
명병은 싸를 없어
출발

2. *Become a brand new person in Christ Jesus.* Previous
to my becoming a brand new person in Christ Jesus, at age
15, I was a very poor student in school. I attended school to
play football, basketball and baseball and to make it difficult
for the teachers. Year after year, I passed by the skin of my
teeth; mostly, I think, because the teachers could not bear the
thought of having me in their class for another year. Then, in
the summer of '53, it happened. I invited Jesus Christ to
come into my life and experienced what the Bible calls the
"new birth." Second Corinthians 5:17, says that when
someone becomes a Christian he becomes a brand new
person inside. He is not the same anymore. A new life has
begun!

예 있는
꿈이서
즉깨드리고
새로운
각오로하여
서론
출발

As I returned to school in the Fall, for my sophomore year,
a whole new world of learning opened up to me. Instead of
being a very poor student, I became an honor student in a
very short time, and by the end of the year was elected to the
National Honor Society. What transformed a poor student
into a good student? It was a result of my becoming a brand
new person in Christ.

Ever since that moment when I committed my life to Jesus,

내 적인 명령

He has been at work helping me to eliminate that which is ugly and unlovable from my life and to develop the best within me.

Give your life to Jesus and let Him eliminate that which is ugly and you do not like; and, with His help, light up the good, fine and beautiful which is within you. It is Christ who takes persons who have the potential to be either good or bad and makes them truly good men and women. Jesus is the Great Restorer of human value. The value of your life goes up when you follow Jesus.

3. *Put your best foot forward*. The way you groom, dress, and present yourself effects your feeling of self-worth. Last spring, when I accepted a speaking engagement which was bigger than anything I had done before, I found myself lacking in self-confidence. My sensitive, tuned-in wife responded to my need by buying me some really sharp looking new clothes to wear. I put them on, looked in the mirror and really felt good about what I was wearing. When it came time in a few days for me to leave for the speaking engagement, I put my new clothes on, looked in the mirror and again felt good feelings about my appearance. This gave me some of the added self-confidence that I needed to rise to the challenge.

Scientific research has proved that when kids are dressed up to look their best, they behave their best. It has been my observation, in working with scores of people, that those who do not put their best foot forward in grooming, manners and presenting themselves do not feel worth much. It is a pity to sell yourself short!

Can you remember in your courting years what you did when you wanted to impress a person of the opposite sex? You didn't do it by showing your worst side, but you made every effort to present yourself in a good light; and because you gave your best, you felt good about yourself. People always feel better about themselves when they are putting their best foot forward. The one thing every person can do to feel better about himself is to put his best foot forward.

4. *Do whatever you can do to improve yourself.* It has been our privilege during the past five years to have two of the reigning Miss America's, Terri Ann Meeuwisen and Shirley Cochran, as guest speakers at our church. As my wife and I have taken these lovely ladies out for dinner, we have observed something very interesting. Each time we have taken Miss America to one of the choice places to eat in our city and repeatedly the young lady of the hour has passed up eating a scrumptious meal to eat like a bird. These girls intentionally disciplined their eating in order to keep themselves in top shape.

Now admittedly few of us have the natural beauty of a Miss America but we all have our own kind of beauty that can be brought out by discipline. Discipline is such a substantial part of developing good feelings about yourself. It is the one thing that no other person can do for you. Without discipline, as someone has said, "we are hell-bent on going nowhere." Discipline is the means whereby a person denies the lesser to gain the greater.

Why not make up your mind to do whatever you need to do to bring out your best. If it's your body that needs shaped up, then go on a diet and exercise program—not tomorrow, but today. I have known people who hated themselves for being fat. Their self-hatred marred their attitude and relationships. Then I've watched them make up their mind to do something about it—go on a diet, exercise, shape their body up. It's always fun to see an overweight person become thin. Maybe that's the reason I have done it so many times in my life. But the more amazing miracle is what happens to that person's

자아의식
Reading

선용지성 에
30세에 고등학업 받여서고
pass etc.
원간 승리의 이야기들

self-esteem. The good feelings that begin to come to the surface. The new glow in their facial expressions. The sparkling beauty in their eyes that tells you, "Hey, I'm an O.K. person."

The other day I heard Elton Trueblood, one of the great minds of our day, challenge an entire student body to expand their minds through reading. So many people today never read a book. They limit their world to such a small space. Working and watching television is about the sum total of their lives. What a small existence. There is a big world out there. You may be trapped by circumstances. You may live in a small town. You may have an inferior education. But you can break through the barriers of time, space and everything else by reading good books. By reading worthwhile books you can expand your horizons. Do what you need to do to sharpen your mind and feel good about yourself.

Joe Flores is one of the special people in our fellowship. Joe's a lot of fun to be around. Joe tells how he was raised in the streets of the inner city of Detroit. His young life was a rough one, without love and filled with trouble. At an early age he dropped out of school. Years later, close to the thirty year mark, with Christ transforming his life and values, Joe made up his mind that he wanted to improve himself. Thus, he quit a full-time job and went back to school. The going was tough but he kept at it. After a lot of dedicated effort, Joe passed all the tests and was awarded his high school diploma. Denying himself to get his high school education completed was but preparation for the training he is now taking in one of the best barber colleges in the Northwest. Joe is denying himself, preparing to fulfill his beautiful dream of having his own barbershop—a barbershop that will be a shining light of witness for Jesus Christ. Joe would tell you himself, that in the past he hasn't felt very good about himself as a person; but with Christ's

고전 9:27

"내가 내몸을 쳐 복종하게 함은 내가 남에게
전파한 후에 자기가 도리어 버림이 될까
두려워 함이로라."

... FEEL GOOD ABOUT YOURSELF/123

※ 최고의 삶에 필요한 최고의 노력

help, as he worked at improving himself, he is experiencing good feelings about himself as a person.

You cannot have the best thing in life unless you are willing to put forth the effort to discipline your mind, your body and your soul. A challenge for us all is to deny the lesser to gain the greater. There is a wonderful you, just waiting to be improved. You owe it to yourself to develop and become the best *you* possible. You have tremendous potential if only you will, with Christ's help, discipline yourself. Nothing great is ever gained in life without discipline, discipline, discipline—and you are the only one who can discipline yourself. Here is testimony from the famous apostle Paul, as written in 1 Corinthians 9:27: "Like an athlete I punish my body, treating it roughly, training it to do what it should, not what it wants to . . ." (*TLB*).

5. *Be true to your highest ideal.* To feel good about yourself you must have self-respect. A lot of people in our society are destroying their own self-respect by doing what they know to be wrong instead of living right. Loose living makes self-esteem go flat like a deflated tire. You can't live like a pig and feel good about it. A young lady wanted to know why she felt so cheap and used. The answer was simple: it was because she kept having sex outside of marriage. Everyone else may be doing it, but if you go against your highest ideals, you are going to feel crumby for doing so. Low living results in low self-esteem. While living up to your highest ideals, you will build your self-esteem.

Arthur Berry was a very famous jewel thief who practiced his trade back in the roaring 20s. He was a very unusual thief in that he would only steal from the very rich. Not only did they have to be rich, but they had to be of the elite rich. The story goes that Arthur would pass up many jewels and take only the finest, most precious. He was one thief that was a

1920년대 Arthur Berry 라는 보석 도둑

상위 계층 가정만을 선택으로 에서 보변류

영박하는 났는 선다가 의늦게 라거가보였을때

훔쳐갔을때

" 누구한테서 가장 큰 건수를 올렸는가 ? "

" 가장 크게 도둑을 맞은 사람은
바로 나자신이다 ... "

내손을 손스로
도둑을 하면서
보낸다
그것

connoisseur of art. Since Arthur Berry stole only from the highest elite of society it became something of a social status to have been robbed by this notorious robber. This kind of wide spread popularity gave the police nightmares.

Well, one day Arthur stole one too many times because the police caught him in the act, and he was shot. While he was suffering excruciating pain he promised himself that he would never steal again. Now, that was a good beginning; but, for some strange happening, Arthur escaped his imprisonment and spent three more years on the loose. Then came his downfall, when an insanely jealous woman turned on him by telling the police where he was. He was recaptured and spent the next eighteen years behind bars. While in prison, Arthur made up his mind that crime didn't pay and that he would never steal again.

When Arthur got out of prison he made his way to a little town up in New England and settled down. People did not suspect that he was a famous jewel thief, and due to his hard work and neighborliness, he soon became one of the small towns respected citizens.

All went well with Arthur until someone came to the little town and recognized him as the famous jewel thief. As the news spread as to who he was, reporters came rushing in from the largest city newspapers to interview this reformed criminal. One of the questions that was put to Arthur by a young reporter was this one: "Arthur, we know that you have taken from some of the wealthiest people in the world. Do you remember who it was that you stole the most from?" Without a moment's hesitation Arthur answered, "The person that I stole the most from was Arthur Berry. I could have made a contribution to society. I could have been a stock broker. I could have been a teacher. I could have been a successful businessman. I could have done all of these, but instead I spent two-thirds of my adult life in prison. I have spent a lifetime robbing myself."

Whenever we go against our highest ideals and compromise ourselves, we rob our ownselves of one of the most precious of inner values, that of self-respect. A person may think they are cheating on their mate, they may think they're cheating other people to get to the top; but in the end, whenever a man or a woman goes against their highest ideals, there is no one they rob of so much as their ownself. Jesus put it this way: "For what shall it profit a man, if he shall gain the whole world, and lose his own soul?" (Mark 8:36, *KJV*).

Some years ago, in another city, I counseled with a young couple by the name of Pete and Sandra. Once they had been in love, but they had drifted away from God and from each other. Now it looked like they would be splitting the sheets unless a miracle happened.

At one time they had the advantage of attending Christian school together where they had shared many wonderful dreams for a Christian ministry. Yet somewhere along the line they got sidetracked and bogged down in a mire of mixed-up values. I guess it all started when Pete, who was a gifted musician, started compromising his Christian values by playing with a band in a very loose, local nightclub. One year before he joined this secular band he never would have dreamed of participating in such a far-out life-style.

Apparently this young man had been resisting all of his wife's appeals to clean up his act. All the while he keeps rationalizing, telling himself that it isn't so bad. The truth is that his wife has lost her respect for him as a spiritual leader and husband. During our conversations I finally got him to open up and admit that, worst of all, he had lost contact with God and respect for himself because of this compromise that he had made.

When he asked me what he should do, with compassion and concern, I said, "Follow this simple rule. Find out what's right and do it, and it will turn out right." Then I added, "But if you persist in doing the wrong, there is no way that it is ever going to turn out right for you."

For a long time he kept trying to resist the truth, kept rationalizing that it wasn't all that bad; and then finally he broke down, confessing to himself, to his wife and to me that ever since that first day when he compromised himself and started playing in the nightclub, his life and marriage had been deteriorating.

Quickly I pointed out this crucial point. I said, "Pete, it took a decision for you to get into this mess, and it is going to take a decision for you to get out of it. Things are not going to change by wishful thinking, or are they going to change by procrastination. The time to do something is now."

Peter made a decision to stop doing what was wrong and with God's help, do what was right. His decision was to immediately quit the band. At that moment of saying, "Yes, Lord, I will do what I know is right," there came into that room a wonderful flow of spiritual renewal, marriage renewal and a renewal of self-respect. I saw them a few years later with their little two-year-old boy. They were as happy as any family I've ever seen.

To live true to your highest ideals in the unclean society we live in, means stepping out from the crowd. Remember, one candle surrounded by darkness is of infinite worth. The Son of God, Jesus, said that you are to be the light of the world. The man, Shakespeare, wrote, "To thine own self be true." Far more important than being accepted by the crowd or achieving worldly success is to be true to your highest ideals and please God. When a person has his values straight he sees that these are one and the same. Do this and self-respect will be your constant companion.

이성, 양심에게성   진실을 주구

여자선이 느그끼가를 말씀기억합시다.

Joseph was a handsome, healthy young Hebrew man. When Joseph arrived in Egypt as a slave he was purchased by Potiphar who was captain of the king's bodyguards. The Lord greatly blessed Joseph in the home of his master, so that everything he did succeeded. Potiphar was so pleased with Joseph, and recognized his special ability, that he put him in charge over all of his household and business affairs.

Potiphar had a wife who was typical of much of our society today. This female was shameless, accommodating, without loyalty, selfish and living life on the low, fleshly level. She was not much more than an animal in the pursuit of her passions. This lewd woman set out to lure Joseph into committing immorality with her. She openly tantalized him and then in hot pursuit invited him to come take her to bed.

Joseph, as a man of God, lived life on a higher level. Things like honesty, loyalty, righteousness, reason and putting God first meant more to Joseph than a fleeting moment of immorality. He said, "How can I do such a wicked thing as this? It would be a great sin against God" (Genesis 39:9, *TLB*).

When his employer's wife sought to seduce him, he might have rationalized it this way: "If I do not give in to her demands, she will get me into trouble. Survival is important and I don't want this scheming woman to become my enemy." And besides, there was his own ever present sex drive to support such a rationalization. Joseph, faced with the greatest of temptations, refused to forget who he was. He rejected her advances. Then, as now, "Hell has no fury like a woman scorned." She raised a cry, claiming that he had tried to rape her. Joseph ended up in jail.

Now prison is a lonely place to be. Although I have never been there, I think it would be the worst place in the world to end up. In ancient Egypt it was a rotten place. Prison life was hard, but Joseph knew one thing, he was innocent; and he slept every night with a clear conscience. He had something that was of priceless value—he had his self-respect, he had done nothing wrong. If this injustice against him was never straightened out, he at least knew inside that he had been true to acting like a king's kid. In prison he could live with himself and love himself for doing right. Wherever we go we have to live with ourselves. Self-respect is worth so much more than the fleeting moments of sinful indulgence. To know that you are living in a way and manner that pleases God is worth more than all the sexy saunas in this world. So, stand up tall like a king's kid, and live clean in an unclean world and enjoy the priceless feeling of self-respect.

6 Love life and it will love you back. What you give is what you get. Love life and life will love you back. Jesus said, "For if you give, you will get!" (Luke 6:38, TLB). Arthur Gordon said, "Fall in love with life—and thereby set in motion the mysterious dynamics that cause life to love you right back." Life is like a boomerang—what you throw out is what comes back to you.

The unwise person views life as one problem after another. While the wise person sees life as a rare privilege with one splendid opportunity after another. Life holds unlimited possibilities for achievement and wonderful opportunities for your enrichment.

It seems to me that all the people in the world are divided into two camps: the spectators and the participators. The spectators are the ones who sit on the sidelines, withholding themselves from life. Is it any wonder that life passes them by? While the participators throw themselves fullheartedly into the action. Whatever it is that's worth doing, they give it all they've got. What you give is what you get.

To me, love is an action word. If you really love someone you don't sit around and speculate about it, but you act like

나는 먼저 치켜세워줄때 나 자신이
치킴을 받는다.

it. You do things which show your love. There is so much in our world to enjoy and love. There are the lakes, the mountains, all of the outdoors with its reaching sky. There are so many good things that need to be done in our world. Find something that needs to be done and start doing it. Throw yourself wholeheartedly into it. Love life and it will love you back.

7. *Lift yourself by first lifting others.* Man's most negative problem is selfishness. Selfishness brings the worst out of a person. It robs him of fulfilling relationships. It isolates him and results in acute loneliness. A man never really finds himself until he somehow gets beyond his own hurts, desires and self-interest. The Master, Jesus, taught that it was only when a man lost himself that he found himself. This is the heart of Christianity and is the heart of generating good feelings about yourself as a person. You lift yourself by first lifting others.

Loneliness is an aching problem to a lot of people today. At some time the persistent lonely person has made up his mind, either consciously or unconsciously, that other people are just not worth putting himself out for. Those who hold back by saying, "I don't want to get hurt," or for whatever reason, live only for themselves and reap the solitude of loneliness. God never intended for anyone to live an isolated, lonely life. He made us social beings to enjoy the fellowship together.

A noble woman lived on the edge of a little midwestern town. Her grown children lived in other states with their families. Alone, she lived isolated half a mile from the nearest house. One day she was asked by a concerned friend if she was lonely. She smilingly replied that she didn't have time for such things, then added her antidote. She said, "Anytime the feeling of loneliness starts, I bake a pie and take it to someone who is ill. Or, I go and baby-sit the neighbor's children.'' What this dear lady had discovered is worth a million dollars. She knew that by committing an act of compassion she was freed from loneliness.

Compassion is one healing, uplifting gift that God has given to each of us to use. An act of warm compassion can break the chains that bind us and hold us down, can transform a cold, indifferent world into a warm, friendly one.

There are so many people around all of us who need the word of encouragement, the smile, the lift, the help that we can give them. But much greater than the other person's need to receive is our own need to give. Everytime you give a lift, you get a lift.

Put other people down and you're going to feel put down. Build other people up and you are going to feel built up. A sure way to build your own self-esteem is to do everything that you can do to help other people succeed and feel good about themselves. The more you care about others, the more alive you are going to become and experience the truth of what Jesus meant when he said, ''My purpose is to give life in all its fullness'' (John 10:10, *TLB*).

8. *Do something greater than you have ever done before*. Young or old, everyone has the same urgent need to feel needed and useful. One of the things I believe so strongly is that God wants to use every person to help others and to make this a better world to live in.

Let's take a look in the Scriptures and try and see if we can answer this question: ''Who does God use?'' It is absolutely dumbfounding, how He used the weak to do some of the strongest things; how He chooses the ordinary to be used to accomplish the extraordinary.

얀 졸다 얀일 겁에서
아직 다 아빠 거룩 도찬의 세계로 [!]

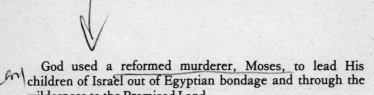

모세 God used a reformed murderer, Moses, to lead His children of Israel out of Egyptian bondage and through the wilderness to the Promised Land.

아브라함 God used a couple right at the age of 100, by the name of Abraham and Sarah, to have a son and become the father and mother of a great nation.

다윗 God used a little boy named David and his little slingshot to do what the great armies of Israel were afraid to do. The little boy, being used by God, not only faced the giant in battle, but defeated him!

어부들 Jesus used common, unlearned fishermen to become His first disciples, to set them on fire to really turn the world upside-down for God!

소년떡? Jesus used a little boy with a few loaves and fishes to work the impossible miracle of multiplication—to feed more than 5,000 hungry people and their families.

베드로 Jesus used a fickle-hearted Peter to become the rock upon which He built His church.

Jesus used an untamed and unridden donkey for His last big joyride into Jerusalem, that the Scripture calls the "triumphant entry."

마가 God used a man by the name of John Mark, who bounced back from failure, to write the Gospel according to Saint Mark.

요한 God used a man by the name of John, who in his early life had an uncontrollable temper and was called the son of Thunder, to show us the depths and the heighths and widths of God's love in action.

바울 God used a converted, zealous persecutor of Christians to be His pioneer missionary and writer of thirteen books in our New Testament, when He called upon Paul.

I have been out of college and seminary for more years than it seems possible. Whenever I hear of, or encounter some of my classmates, what a surprise it is! For example, one young man—who as the Number 1 "goof-off" and certainly not much of a student all the way through our schooling—is currently being used to lead an outstanding ministry today. *What unlikely people God so often uses to do His greatest work.*

WHO DOES GOD USE?
HE USES PEOPLE LIKE YOU AND ME.

Whatever you do, don't allow past failures to defeat you and stop you before you get started. Failure is a tough teacher, but a good one. When you have learned your lessons from it, you are better prepared than ever before to move ahead and do something great with your life.

If God can take the failures in a minister's life, like mine, and help me to turn them into a need-meeting ministry of new hope to multitudes of people; then you, too, can do something greater than you have ever done before.

There is something you've been wanting to do. If you wait until you have just the right set of circumstances before you decide to do it, the time given to you in your life will pass by and you will never do it. The saddest words of all, I think, are: "It might have been."

If there is something you've been wanting to do—it's a great thing for God, it's going to help other people and bring the best out in you—then do it! Seize the opportunity that is yours. Do something greater than you've ever done before, and I know from my own experience that you are going to feel good about yourself again as a person.

WHY NOT?

이럴 수 있겠는데~~

9

❦

Reach Out to
New Horizons

9

During a recent Christmas season, my Uncle George Galloway and Aunt Martha came for a family visit for a few days. In one of the conversations that my uncle and I enjoyed, he told me about his son-in-law who was in the United States Navy, stationed in San Diego. This young Navy man is assigned to a new multi-million dollar ship.It stretched my mind when my uncle related that this ship is more than 900 feet long. Think of it, that's three football fields long. Because of the immensity of this floating giant, it takes a crew of 1,600 men to operate it.

This particular ship is the pride of the naval fleet. It has the latest and most up-to-date equipment and application of our most advanced scientific know-how. It's crew has spent hours in training and preparation to properly handle and operate it to maximum efficiency. When it comes to sailing to any destination in the world, it can do it. But suppose this huge naval ship just sat at the dock, day after day, and never shipped out to go anywhere; never received any orders to sail to a destination. What a waste this would be! It would be one of the most extravagant wastes of potential power and available personnel that has ever happened in modern times.

Without a goal, we become like that ship—sitting at the dock, with potential to go anywhere, but going nowhere.

What a waste to sit, day after day, going nowhere when you could be reaching to new horizons.

Six years ago I was like that ship sitting at the dock, going absolutely nowhere. With the help of God, I had somehow managed to survive the hell of my divorce and all of the ugly fallout. For months life for me had been at its lowest ebb, where it was a big thing just to survive one more day. But as I cooperated with God's work within me, wholeness began to replace my brokenness. Let me tell you, God specializes in making the broken whole.

A large part of the inner healing in my own life was the love that God brought into my life through the friendship and marriage of Margi. Although enjoying the springtime of our love so much, I still found myself restless. Why? Because like you, I needed a dream to give the lift to my life.

Whenever a person has a dream, something happens inside of him that ignites the spark of life. A person possessed with a dream wakes up in the morning with excitement and expectation for the day. What a difference between the person who has a dream and one who doesn't. A person with a dream lives anything but a boring life while a person without a dream drifts through life and is often bored. The person with a dream has an inner motivation that gives zest and energy to life, while the person without a dream works out of duty and has a low energy level.

To me there is nothing worse than to live without a dream. Without a lifting dream, life becomes like a fishing reel with the drag on. It is a drag to even get out of bed.

One day, as I was talking to God about my restlessness, I opened my mind to dream a new dream. As I was sharing with God, as we were dreaming together, I was led to read these words from the book of Isaiah which Jesus read in the Synagogue at the launching of his own public ministry: "The Spirit of the Lord is upon me; he has appointed me to preach

Good News to the poor; he has sent me to heal the brokenhearted and to announce that captives shall be released and the blind shall see, that the downtrodden shall be freed from their oppressors, and that God is ready to give blessings to all who come to him'' (Luke 4:18, 19, *TLB*).

In that holy moment, God placed a magnificent new dream in my mind and heart. To me the Spirit of the Lord said, ''Son, I am not finished with your life yet. I am just preparing you to be used to lead a ministry of new hope to the unchurched thousands. I want you to take my love to all those who are down, beaten, bruised and broken. I want you to tell them there is hope. That I, God, specialize in new beginnings. And just as I have, this day, given you a new dream of new hope, I want you to give new hope to all of those who for one reason or another have lost hope.''

New Hope's beginning happened on October 14, 1972. On that anxious day we opened the gates of a drive-in theater on 82nd Street in Portland. Margi and I climbed up a shaky ladder, walked the 100 feet across the roof, and stood on top of the snackshack to sing and preach to those first pioneers that came to our drive-in church in their cars. Since, I have come to believe the words of my friend, Bob Schuller, when he said to me, ''Dale, there are infinite possibilities in small beginnings.''

What God has done with that original step of faith is staggering. To us He has given beautiful dear friends, a ministry of hope and healing that is now reaching into the thousands and multiplying daily. God has used our faith—put into positive action—to give His healing, lifting, and transforming love to so many. The miracle of New Hope goes on and on. To God be the glory for the miracles that are happening because we dare to reach to new horizons.

My friend, you too can dream a new dream. No matter who you are; no matter what your age is; or no matter what has happened to you: *You can dream a beautiful new dream!* Go ahead and let your God-given imagination run wild. It doesn't cost one dime to dream. A dream is what you need to:

> Revive you,
> Lift you,
> Inspire you,
> Excite you,
> Motivate you,
> To reach to new horizons.

Before you can arrive at a new horizon you have got to decide where it is you want to go. To every person God has given the marvelous ability of visualization. You have the ability to see where it is you want to go, and to set out to go to that exact destination point. But it is up to you to set your aim! There is no winning of the game without first setting the aim.

J.C. Penny put the thread through the needle's point when he said, "Give me a stock clerk with a goal, and I will give you a man who will make history. Give me a man without a goal, and I will give you a stock clerk."

Who needs goals? Everyone needs goals. The young, the older, the male, the female. The man who wants the best and the man who gets the best has to have a goal. Functionally, we are all like bicycles: unless we are moving forward towards a goal, we are going to flounder and fall. It is only with a goal that you are going to go forward and achieve the things that you want most out of life. In setting goals that will lift you to new horizons, there are these—

EIGHT THINGS YOU NEED TO KNOW:

1. *Choose worthwhile goals.* I counseled with a man once who had a goal that he was really set on. But, I wouldn't call it a very worthwhile goal. As a matter of fact, it proved to be

a very devastating and destructive one. His goal was to steal his neighbor's wife. This he achieved, and it destroyed and devastated two families.

To get the very best out of life, it is important not only to set goals but to be selective in the goals that you choose for yourself. One of my problems in the past, in goal setting, was that I didn't make love my number one aim. May I again suggest to you, out of my bitter experience, that the first and number one goal for a successful life is to make love your number one aim.

I am finding that when I keep the priority of love first in my life, above all other goals, that this alone keeps me on the beam in reaching for true success instead of the kind that can crumble in your hands. In selecting a goal, I like to ask myself three questions: Would this be a great thing for God? Would this help hurting people? And lastly, would this bring the best out of me?

Here are some goals that you will want to consider and set for yourself: your relationship with God; family goals; vocational goals; personal goals (things like exercise, change of habits); financial goals[5]; ministry goals; and church goals.

2. *Goals that you choose should be tailor-made and realistic.* When I reached for a new horizon by setting my goal to build New Hope Community Church, although it was a stretching experience for me, it also was realistic. Although I didn't have money or backing, I had something more important—I had wisdom and experience of know-how, having started a church in my first pastorate. On the other hand, for a middle-aged man with heavy financial and family responsibilities, who had no prior practical experience, to go out and start a brand new church, could be a very foolish

5. Here you might like to read my writings on setting financial goals, included in my book *There Is a Solution to Your Money Problems* (Regal, (1977)).

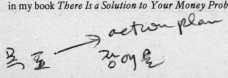

Big enough to challenge + stretch

thing to do.

3. *Set your sights on something big enough to challenge the best in you.* Time and again in the sports world we see the number one-ranked team in the nation knocked off by an unrated team. How can an average football team, for example, knock off the top college team in the nation on any given Saturday? It is because athletes perform at their best against tough competition, while they don't come up to par against easier competition. It takes a challenging goal to make us stretch and reach. I like to set goals that are going to bring the best out of me, to stir my blood, to bring excitement to my daily life. What do you say? Make your goals big enough to make you bounce out of bed in the morning and put your best foot forward throughout the day. That way it is fun to be alive! This is one big reason why "I'd rather attempt something great for God and fail than to do nothing and succeed."

4. *When setting your goal—look at what you want to accomplish—not at the obstacles.* I hate to admit it, but I almost killed New Hope Community Church before it was born. Yes, God had given me a beautiful dream. I had the goal of building a ministry to reach unchurched thousands. But then I got my eyes on the giant obstacles. They scared me. They looked so impossible. I feared failure. So many of my friends thought that it was a foolish thing for me to do. Obstacles, obstacles, defeating obstacles.

Then one day I looked at Jesus, my source of total supply, and I saw that with Him, the impossible is possible. I fixed my sights on the goal, and, at that moment, my entire frame of mind changed from negative to positive. The promise of God is true: "According to your faith be it (done) unto you" (Matthew 9:29, *KJV*).

As you set your goals, let me urge you not to attempt to

overcome the obstacles before you start. Nobody—but nobody—would ever attempt anything of significance if all obstacles had to be removed before they started.

I heard the other day about a man who had to go across town to work, so the first thing he did when he got up in the morning, was call the sheriff's office to inquire if all of the lights would be green on his way to work. He decided that if they would all be green—he would go to work. The sergeant who answered the phone thought that the phone caller was under the influence, and hung up on him.

We laugh at this man's foolishness, and yet how many times we let a few red lights stop us from moving ahead. How do you travel from one side of the city to another, when you know you are going to encounter many red lights along the way? You do it by taking one light at a time, and after awhile, you overcome all of the obstacles and arrive at your destination.

You can expect some obstacles along the way. The greater your goal, the bigger your obstacles. Someone has said, "You measure the size of the accomplishment by the obstacles you have to overcome to reach your goal."

5. *Goals must be specific.* If your goal is "to at some time, buy a house," that is not a specific goal, but an almost meaningless generality. On the other hand, if you make it your goal that: in a set year, you are going to buy a three-bedroom house, with two baths, a double garage, and in the price range of $40,000 in the suburb of Milwaukee—that is getting specific.

I wonder how many of you ever owned a magnifying glass when you were growing up. If you didn't have a magnifying glass, you never lived! I can remember those hot summers in Columbus, Ohio, when I would go out in the backyard with my magnifying glass and hold it up for the sunlignt to penetrate through it. I'd hold the glass real still, and focus it on the twigs. As I did that, the power of the sun would penetrate and, to my boyhood merriment, a roaring fire would start.

But if I kept moving the magnifying glass from one place to another I never got the desired results. In order to accomplish, you've got to concentrate. *Zero in on a goal.* Too many people spend their lives jumping all around, and never really sticking to anything long enough to make it happen.

6. *Set a date and get started.* Someone has said, "Beginning is half done." Every week I write a sermon for publication for a large mailing list. This is something that I plan to accomplish every week. Do you know the most difficult part of the sermon for me to write? It is the introduction. When I get the introduction done, I feel like I have half the sermon finished, even though I've just begun. The hardest part of anything is just getting started. Whatever it takes for you to get started, do it without further delay. Write that letter, go see the person you need to see, start gathering the facts. Take action now!

7. *Break your large goal into small parts.* I have a friend (and since I would like to keep him as my friend, I won't mention his name here) who I really think could eat a whole pie at one sitting. I mean he really loves to eat pie. Whenever we are together, he is always wanting to stop at a pie shop and, believe me, he knows where the best pie is in town. Now I like to eat pie also, but I don't think I could eat a whole pie at one sitting. However, I could take a pie, cut it into seven pieces, and eat one piece each day of the week. At the end of the week, my goal of eating the entire pie would be reached.

8. *To achieve a goal—you must deny the lesser to gain the greater.* This past winter I finally faced up to the fact that I had allowed myself to get twenty pounds overweight. I guess I had eaten too many pies with my friend. My problem is that

?

I love to eat food, it tastes so good. You know, I think just about everyone would agree that eating is a good thing. My problem, like a lot of yours, comes from eating too much. Before I lost the twenty pounds and got myself back into good shape, I had to decide that I wanted to lose weight more than I wanted to eat. Once I set my mind that I had to deny the lesser (of eating) to gain the greater (of being in good physical shape), it wasn't many months until the goal was achieved. The Bible says it this way: "To win the contest you must deny yourselves many things that would keep you from doing your best" (1 Corinthians 9:25, *TLB*).

One final lesson about goal-setting. Ask yourself this question: Are you driven, or driving? The answer will make quite a difference in your life, and in the lives of the ones whom you live with. For many years in my goal-setting and drive for success, I was driven by my goals. This resulted in tension in my life, and often being insensitive and unresponsive to the needs of loved ones and people around me. In reaching for your goals, don't make the mistake of living all in the out there, and not relating to, and enjoying, the now.

It is a good feeling to have reached a point in life where I am learning to set worthwhile goals, and then be the master and manager of those goals, instead of becoming the slave and to keep reaching beyond to new horizons and yet enjoying each precious day to the fullest for what it is.

What relished things come into the lives of those who keep reaching for new horizons. People who live in the spirit of adventure are fun to be around. They are the ones who overcome their fears of failure with faith and, with God's help, reach beyond through the unknown to new splendid horizons.

Right after we started the ministry of New Hope, Carol Montag, one of our very creative members, made me a large green turtle. When she gave it to me, on it was pinned these words, "Behold the turtle! He makes progress only when he sticks his neck out."

I am convinced that God put the turtle on the earth, if for nothing else, to teach you and me an unforgettable lesson. Look at the turtle! Until he comes out of his shell and sticks his neck out, he goes absolutely nowhere. What a lesson for us to learn. Until we stick our necks out, we do not advance.

At sometime or other, everyone of us fails, and the runaway feeling is to put our necks back in our shells and stay put. As you know, this is a dull way to live. Besides, if a person chooses to play it safe and stays where he is, there is no way he is going to advance. Believe it, God has something greater for you to do. He has a new plateau for you to reach. He has a new blessing to bring into your life. Right now, without further delay, replace fear of failure with faith in God. Stick your neck out and begin to move ahead to capture new horizons.

When I stop to think where I would be today if I had stayed in my shell, licked my wounds, wallowed around in my failure, been satisfied to live in a failure situation in which I found myself, I am filled with thanksgiving to God who put the desire within me for something greater, who gave me the faith and the courage to reach beyond to new horizons. This is the same thing that God wants to do for you. But you have got to step out of the shell of past failures and reach forward to new horizons. Believe me, a person with forward motion is going somewhere.

May these words, that have come to mean so much to me, become your heartbeat:

"Grieve not for me, about to start a new adventure
Eager I stand, and ready to depart
Me and my reckless pioneer heart."

—Author unknown

Now, move ahead to reach for new horizons, and feel good about yourself.